Knitting by Nature

19 Patterns for Scarves, Wraps, and More

SHERYL THIES

Martingale®
Create with Confidence

❧ Dedication: for Kevin ❧

CREDITS

President & CEO: Tom Wierzbicki
Editor in Chief: Mary V. Green
Design Director: Paula Schlosser
Managing Editor: Karen Costello Soltys
Technical Editor: Amy Polcyn
Copy Editor: Sheila Chapman Ryan
Production Manager: Regina Girard
Cover & Text Designer: Adrienne Smitke
Illustrator: Robin Strobel
Photographer: Brent Kane

Mission Statement

Dedicated to providing quality products and service to inspire creativity.

Knitting by Nature: 19 Patterns for Scarves, Wraps, and More
© 2012 by Sheryl Thies

Martingale®
Create with Confidence

Martingale®
19021 120th Ave. NE, Ste. 102
Bothell, WA 98011-9511 USA
ShopMartingale.com

Printed in China
17 16 15 14 13 12   8 7 6 5 4 3 2 1

Library of Congress Cataloging-in-Publication Data is available upon request.

ISBN: 978-1-60468-155-0

Contents

Planting and Sprouting the Seed 4
Groundwork 5

PROJECTS

Planting and Sprouting the Seed

If you're like me, you eagerly wait for that first spring day that's warm enough to open a window. I always roll up my sleeves, slip on a pair of sandals, and head outside to enjoy it. And after a few warm days, the landscape begins to show signs of life—green shoots poke through the dirt and trees start budding. But, faced with the reality of a Wisconsin winter, the wait can be agonizingly long.

Every year, I enjoy a brief reprieve from winter's grip; it arrives early in January, just like clockwork. My respite arrives in my mailbox in the form of a catalog, thanks to the Gurney's Seed and Nursery Company. The oversized spring catalog is a sure sign that winter will eventually end. And until it does, I can drink in the magic of spring with photos of blooms in kaleidoscopic colors, delicate new sprouts and shoots, and fast-growing vines. I relish the fantasies of sweet-tasting fruits, blue-ribbon vegetables, and overgrown woodlands. With page after page of eye-catching foliage, grand trees, flowers for butterflies, vegetables, lush grasses, and wonderful cooking herbs, the winter doldrums don't have a chance.

Before you conjure up the wrong impression of me, I need to confess: I'm rather inept—well, downright incompetent—when it comes to tending plants and gardening. My backyard, canopied by oak trees that define the phrase "deep shade," isn't conducive to growing much more than moss. The healthy and thriving plants in- and outside the house are due to the efforts of my husband, Kevin. Kevin gets all the credit for keeping the trees, herbs, and other plants alive and lush.

That said, my appreciation for plants compensates for my incompetence. My dreams are just as dramatic and my passion as strong as any Master Gardener. I search for the first buds and blooms in spring, and I savor the taste of fresh local vegetables that come in my weekly Community Supported Agriculture (CSA) box. In fall, I love hearing the acorns drop from the tall oaks, hit the roof, and then roll down. I buy ornamental corn at the farmers' market and rake and rake and rake all the colorful leaves that drop in our yard. In winter I appreciate the color that the Blue Spruce provides against the snowy countryside.

One bitterly cold January night, as I was paging through the Gurney's catalog, I felt inspired—the seeds of an idea were planted. After working up several yarn swatches—Red Beets, Brussels Sprout, and Clematis—the seeds definitely sprouted, and I knew I had the concept for this book. I would knit my own version of a perennial garden. Once knit, I could enjoy it year after year.

As I expanded the collection of "plants" and worked my "garden" by knitting scarves, shawls, and shrugs, the winter melted away. And before I knew it the windows were open, my sleeves were rolled up, and I was wearing sandals. Nature once again showed its resilience.

Texture, stitch patterns, and color dominate this collection of scarves, shawls, and shrugs. Mixed with a little subtle shaping, clever accents, and a bit of drape, you have invigorating projects to knit and stylish accessories to wear.

Some of the stitches and techniques used may be new to you, but that doesn't make them hard to master. Many of the patterns have repetitive stitches and are easy to work and memorize. With a little practice you can easily master a new technique and produce beautiful accessories that you'll enjoy year after year.

Start by visiting your local yarn store to select that perfect yarn. If you want your completed project to look like the one in the book, choose the specific yarn or one with similar gauge, fiber, and structure. If you choose a yarn that's markedly different, understand that the end product will also be markedly different—although the result may still be a very attractive and striking garment. The choice is yours.

Reading yarn labels can reduce the unknown of selecting and substituting yarn. The label will state the needle size and gauge, yardage, fiber content, and care instructions. When substituting yarn, you want to pick a yarn that is a similar thickness. To make this selection easier, there are universal symbols indicating yarn weights (thickness). The weight of the yarn used for each project in this book is indicated with a corresponding symbol. Comparing the yarn-weight symbol to the standard yarn-weight chart will identify the type of yarn you should be looking for (see "Yarn-Weight Guidelines" on page 79).

Be sure to purchase a sufficient amount of yarn. The directions, under the heading of "Materials," give the number of skeins for each project and the yardage for each skein. Multiply the number of balls times the amount of yarn on each ball to determine the total number of yards required for the specific wrap. Once you find a yarn that you'd like to use, read the label to determine the yardage for that skein. Divide the total number of yards required by the amount in each ball of the substituted yarn to determine the number of balls you should purchase.

Sometimes you'll have some yarn left over—this is a lot better than running short! If you have ever run short and were unable to purchase enough to complete the project, you understand the importance of buying enough yarn. Also if you want to alter the project to make it larger or longer, remember to purchase more yarn.

There are many stunningly beautiful hand-dyed yarns available. The virtue of hand-dyed yarn is that the colors are not uniform, neither within a skein nor between skeins. There are no dye lots. The variation of color is what makes these skeins so spectacular. If you're working a piece that requires more than one skein, you want the colors to blend and fall evenly through the piece. Rather than working one skein, and then going on to the next, work two rows with one ball, and then two rows with another, alternating every two rows. The unused yarn is carried up the side of the work.

Don't overlook the importance of gauge. The gauge given for each project sometimes won't correspond to the gauge suggested on the yarn label. The stitch pattern greatly affects the number of stitches per inch, and the only way to know if you have the right combination of yarn and needles is to make a gauge swatch—and in some cases make another and another.

The gauge swatch is the perfect way to master the stitch pattern. To make a gauge swatch in a pattern stitch, you want to end up with a knit piece about 4" square. The gauge given as part of the instructions will indicate the number of stitches for 4", but check the pattern-stitch multiple number. If the multiple is nine plus four, cast on 22 stitches (9 x 2 repeats + 4 = 22). This will allow you to work two complete pattern repeats. Work in the pattern until the piece measures 4", or longer if there are more rows to the pattern repeat. Measure the width of the swatch and divide by 22 stitches for the number of stitches per inch. If the number of stitches per inch is less than the desired number, go down a needle size and repeat the pattern. If the number of stitches per inch is more than the desired number, go up a needle size.

All gauges for the projects are given after blocking with the stated blocking method. Stitch patterns before blocking often bunch together and hide the beauty of the pattern. Blocking will open up, spread out, and even out the stitches, giving the proper dimensions to the finished piece. Amazingly, a blocked piece of lace looks completely different from the unblocked piece. Several different methods for blocking are discussed (page 76) and each project specifies a suggested blocking method.

You may have to repeat this process several times to get to the stated stitch gauge. You may feel this is a waste of time; however, don't despair—if you want the project to turn out as described, the proper gauge needs to be achieved. If you want to freelance and try something different, go for it! You may end up with a greatly enhanced and desirable piece of work; however, if it doesn't look like the photo, gauge is probably the culprit.

The good news with gauge is that generally you don't have to deal with row gauge. Since all but one of the patterns are written in inches rather than rows per inch, row gauge is not even specified in the patterns. Violets is the only project with a specific row gauge.

Before going on to the actual project, you may want to work a few more pattern repeats to become more familiar with the techniques used in the pattern stitch. The exact execution of a step will impact the outcome of a piece. For example, *make one* and *yarn over* are two ways of increasing one stitch, but there's a big difference in the result—make one is an almost invisible increase, while the yarn over is an increase that leaves a very noticeable hole.

Many knitters avoid lace stitch patterns, erroneously thinking lace is for experienced knitters only. Understanding the basic elements of lace, as well as simple increases and decreases, will help demystify even the most complex lace pattern. A yarn over (YO), the increase that creates the decorative hole, is balanced with a decrease necessary to maintain the stitch count and shape the lace piece. Decreases may be right slanting or left slanting, and may be made as single or multiple decreases.

Working lace does require good light and appropriate needles. Personal preference comes into play regarding type of needles, such as straight, circular, bamboo, metal, or plastic; however, a pair of needles with nice pointed tips will make manipulating the stitches more manageable and the process more enjoyable.

Look at your knitting often as you work and learn to recognize the various stitches. Being able to identify the yarn overs and left and right decreases will help you find your way if you lose your place. The unblocked lace may be a little bunched up, but you can smooth the fabric with your hands, bringing the stitches into view. This is what is referred to as "reading your knitting." And it's an especially valuable skill to possess.

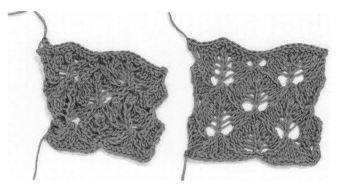

Unblocked and blocked lace swatches

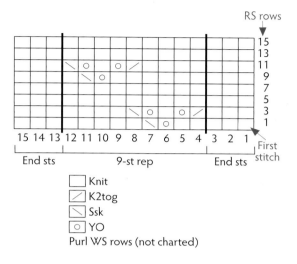

☐ Knit
◻ K2tog
◻ Ssk
◻ YO
Purl WS rows (not charted)

Begin reading chart at bottom right.
Right-side rows read right to left. The
wrong-side rows (even-numbered)
are not shown on this chart.

Charts are provided for most of the stitch patterns, and knowing how to read a chart will complement your ability to read your knitting. Just as reading your knitting gives a visual representation of your knitting, charts provide the visual representation of the pattern. Knitting charts are read beginning with the first row at the bottom. Right-side rows, the odd-numbered rows, are read from right to left. Wrong-side rows, the even-numbered rows, are read from left to right. If a chart doesn't have even rows charted, the pattern is usually a plain purl row. When working in the round, read all chart rows from right to left. Associated with charts are symbols that indicate what is done with each stitch. Many symbols are easy to understand; for example, the yarn over symbol is a O—it looks like the decorative hole that it makes. But be sure to check the symbol key before working to fully understand the stitch that is to be worked. With a little practice, charts are very easy to use and often preferred by knitters.

Several projects have a crocheted edge rather than a knit edge. The various crochet stitches provide a decorative finish and stabilize the edges. For more information, see "Crochet" (page 76). Even for a novice crocheter, the trims can be completed easily and quickly. Use your gauge swatch to practice the edgings.

The projects in this collection—scarves, shawls, and shrugs—are simple shapes that require little or no finishing beyond weaving in ends and blocking. Many have a relatively small number of stitches to work in a row. For these reasons the actual skill level is not noted. If you know how to cast on, knit and purl, and bind off, and the project appeals to you, give it a try. A little practice with the technique and specific stitch pattern should be enough to build your confidence and skill level so that you can successfully complete the project.

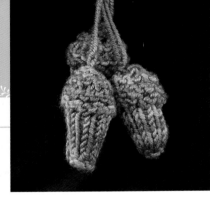

Acorns

Finished Measurements: 17" x 75"

Acorns: The nuts of oak trees. Acorns are believed to symbolize prosperity and success; it's said that good luck will follow if you carry an acorn in your pocket.

Imagine all your good fortune when you wrap up in this luxurious wool-and-silk acorn shawl. Each corner tassel, a cluster of acorns, embellishes and adds a touch more good luck.

Materials

6 skeins of Fingering 55 Silk from Claudia Hand Painted Yarns (55% silk, 45% merino wool; 50 g; 175 yds) in color Urban Fever 〔1〕

Size 7 (4.5 mm) circular needle (24" or longer) or size required to obtain gauge

Size 8 (5 mm) circular needle for casting on

Size 10½ (6.5 mm) needles for binding off

Size 3 (3.25 mm) needles for acorn tassels

Small amount of fiberfill or cotton balls

Tapestry needle

Gauge

4 sts = 1" in acorn lace patt using size 7 needle

Acorn Lace Pattern

(Multiple of 6 + 2 + 10 edge sts)

Note: This pattern is also charted; see page 10.

Row 1 (RS): K6, *K3, P3, rep from * to last 6 sts, end K6.

Row 2: K5, P1,*K3, P3, rep from * to last 6 sts, end P1, K5.

Row 3: K6, *YO, K3tog, YO, K3, rep from * to last 6 sts, end K6.

Row 4: K5, P1, *P3, K1, P1, K1, rep from * to last 6 sts, end P1, K5.

Row 5: K6, *P3, K3, rep from * to last 6 sts, end K6.

Row 6: K5, P1, *P3, K3, rep from * to last 6 sts, end P1, K5.

Row 7: K6, *K3, YO, K3tog, YO, rep from * to last 6 sts, end K6.

Row 8: K5, P1, *K1, P1, K1, P3, rep from * to last 6 sts, P1, K5.

Rep rows 1–8 for patt.

Shawl

With size 8 needle, CO 300 sts. Change to size 7 needle and knit 6 rows. Work setup row as follows: K5, P1, *K3, P3, rep from * to last 6 sts, end P1, K5. Beg acorn lace patt and work until piece measures approx 16" slightly stretched, ending with row 8. Knit 6 rows. With size 10½ needles, BO all sts loosely.

Finishing

Weave in ends. Block using mist-and-pin method (page 76) to smooth and even the sts.

Acorns (make 12):

With size 3 needles, CO 5 sts, leaving approx 12" tail.

Row 1 (RS): K1f&b into each st—10 sts.

Rows 2, 4, 6, and 8: Purl.

Rows 3, 5, and 7: Knit.

Row 9: K1, K1f&b in each st to last st, K1—18 sts.

Rows 10–14: Knit.

Row 15: *K2tog, rep from * to end—9 sts.

Row 16: *K2tog, rep from * to last st, end K1—5 sts.

Cut yarn, leaving 12" tail. With tapestry needle, thread tail through rem sts on needle and pull to gather sts and secure, do not cut yarn. With tail at CO edge, work seam toward the cap (see "Mattress Stitch" on page 75), stuffing lightly. Tie starting and ending tails tog at top of acorn to secure; then tie groups of 3 acorns tog to create tassels. Embellish each corner of wrap by sewing on a 3-acorn tassel.

Green Thumb Tip

Improve your luck even more by making additional acorns and applying them along both short sides like fringe.

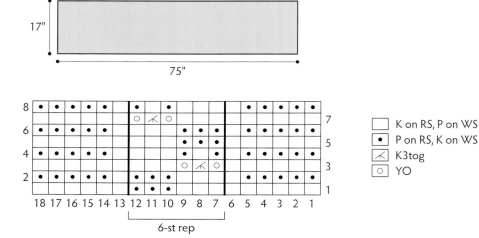

Bean Sprouts

Finished Measurements: Neck edge: 26" Bottom edge: 194" Length: 6"

Bean sprouts: Tender, edible seedlings that are delicious, nutritious, and versatile.

Somewhere between a swirl and a ruffle, this versatile accessory can be worn as a collar that swirls around the neckline or as a ruffled scarf.

Materials

Extra Fine Mohair from Be Sweet (100% baby mohair; 25 g; 230 yds)

1

  A: 1 skein in color Green Potion

  B: 1 skein in color Sand

Size 11 (8 mm) needles or size required to obtain gauge

Size 13 (9 mm) needles for binding off

Tapestry needle

Gauge

10 sts = 4" in St st (exact gauge is not critical)

Bean-Sprout Pattern

(Multiple of 6 + 5 sts)

Row 1 (RS): With A, knit.

Row 2: With A, purl.

Row 3: With B, K2, *sl 1 wyib, K1, rep from * to last st, K1.

Row 4: With B, K1, *(K1, sl 1 wyif) twice, P1, sl 1 wyif, rep from * to last 4 sts, end K1, sl 1 wyif, K2.

Row 5: With A, knit.

Row 6: With A, purl.

Rep rows 1–6 for patt.

Scarf

With size 11 needles and A, CO 65. Knit 2 rows.

Work 6 rows of bean-sprout patt.

Next row (RS): With A, K3, K1f&b in each st to last 2 sts, end K2—125 sts.

With A, knit 1 row.

Work 6 rows of bean-sprout patt.

Next row (RS): With A, K3, K1f&b in each st to last 2 sts, end K2—245 sts.

With A, knit 1 row.

Work 6 rows of bean-sprout patt.

Next row (RS): With A, K3, K1f&b in each st to last 2 sts, end K2—485 sts.

With A, knit 3 rows.

Work 6 rows of bean-sprout patt.

With A, knit 2 rows.

With size 13 needles and B, BO all sts very loosely as follows: Using cable CO (page 73), *CO 2 sts, BO 4, rep from * to end for picot BO.

Finishing

Weave in ends. Block using mist method (page 76) to smooth and even the sts.

Green Thumb Tip

If you bind off the edge too tightly, the edge will pucker and not lie smooth. The picot bind-off technique adds a bit of elasticity to the otherwise inelastic bouclé mohair to help prevent this problem. Using a larger needle makes larger stitches so the edge will ruffle to its fullest potential.

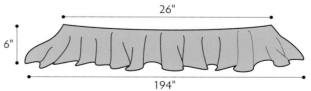

26"

6"

194"

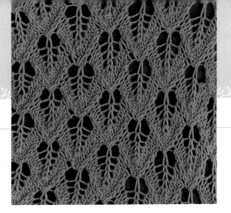

Bleeding Heart

Finished Measurements: 13" x 60" excluding loop closure

Bleeding heart: Open in late spring, the long-lasting, heart-shaped pendant blooms of this plant create a lavish display of color.

This captivating shawl with seed-stitch loop closure and bleeding-heart lace adds a burst of intense color that's not for the faint of heart.

Materials

6 skeins of Snuggly Baby Bamboo DK from Sirdar (80% bamboo sourced viscose, 20% wool; 50 g; 104 yds) in color 158 Rinky Dinky Pink

Size 7 (4.5 mm) circular needle (24") or size required to obtain gauge

Safety pin or removable stitch marker

2 stitch markers

Tapestry needle

Gauge

22 sts = 4" in bleeding-heart patt

Seed Stitch

(Odd number of sts)

Row 1: *K1, P1, rep from * to last st, end K1.

Row 2 and all subsequent rows: Knit the purl sts and purl the knit sts.

Rep row 2 for patt.

Bleeding-Heart Pattern

(Multiple of 12 + 1 sts)

Note: This pattern is also charted; see page 16.

Row 1 (RS): K1, *YO, ssk, K7, K2tog, YO, K1, rep from * to end.

Row 2: *P1, YO, P1, P2tog, P5, P2tog tbl, P1, YO, rep from * to last st, end P1.

Row 3: K1, *YO, K2, ssk, K3, K2tog, K2, YO, K1, rep from * to end.

Row 4: *P1, YO, P3, P2tog, P1, P2tog tbl, P3, YO, rep from * to last st, end P1.

Row 5: K1, *YO, K4, K3tog, K4, YO, K1, rep from * to end.

Row 6: *P4, P2tog tbl, YO, P1, YO, P2tog, P3, rep from * to last st, end P1.

Row 7: K1, *K2, K2tog, K1, YO, K1, YO, K1, ssk, K3, rep from * to end.

Row 8: *P2, P2tog tbl, P2, YO, P1, YO, P2, P2tog, P1, rep from * to last st, end P1.

Row 9: K1, *K2tog, K3, YO, K1, YO, K3, ssk, K1, rep from * to end.

Row 10: P2tog tbl, P4, YO, P1, YO, P4, *P3tog, P4, YO, P1, YO, P4, rep from * to last 2 sts, end P2tog.

Rep rows 1–10 for patt.

Shawl

Loop closure:

CO 37 sts.

Work in seed st (mark RS with safety pin or removable marker) until piece measures 11", ending with WS row.

Joining row (RS): Work 6 seed sts, knit to end of row, do not turn, referring to schematic (below right), curve work to align CO edge and current row so they are side by side. PU 36 sts along CO edge—73 sts.

Body of shawl:

Setup row (WS): Work 6 seed sts, pm, purl to last 6 sts, pm, 6 seed sts.

Work in seed st to marker, work row 1 of bleeding-heart patt to 2nd marker, work seed sts to end. Cont in established patt until piece measures approx 58" or desired length, ending with row 10.

Work 6 seed sts, knit to last 6 sts, end 6 seed sts.

Work 1 row seed st.

Next 4 rows: (Sl1k, BO 4 sts in patt, cont across row in seed st)—57 sts.

Next 8 rows: (Sl1k, BO 6 sts in patt, cont across row in seed st)—9 sts.

Next row: Sl1k, BO rem sts in patt.

Finishing

Weave in ends. Block using wet method (page 76) to smooth and even the sts.

Green Thumb Tip

For a custom fit, you can determine the desired length to work the shawl by measuring around your shoulders and over your upper arms. To this measurement, add the desired length to pass through the loop closure. Remember to purchase extra yarn if you plan on making your shawl longer than the one shown.

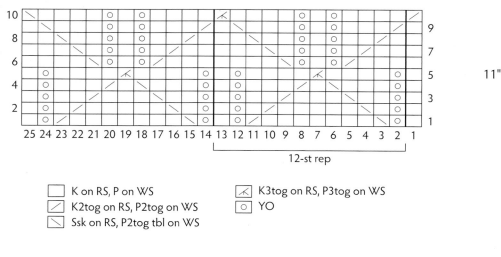

12-st rep

☐	K on RS, P on WS
╱	K2tog on RS, P2tog on WS
╲	Ssk on RS, P2tog tbl on WS
⅄	K3tog on RS, P3tog on WS
○	YO

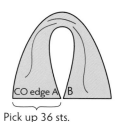

11"

6½"

CO edge A / B

Pick up 36 sts.

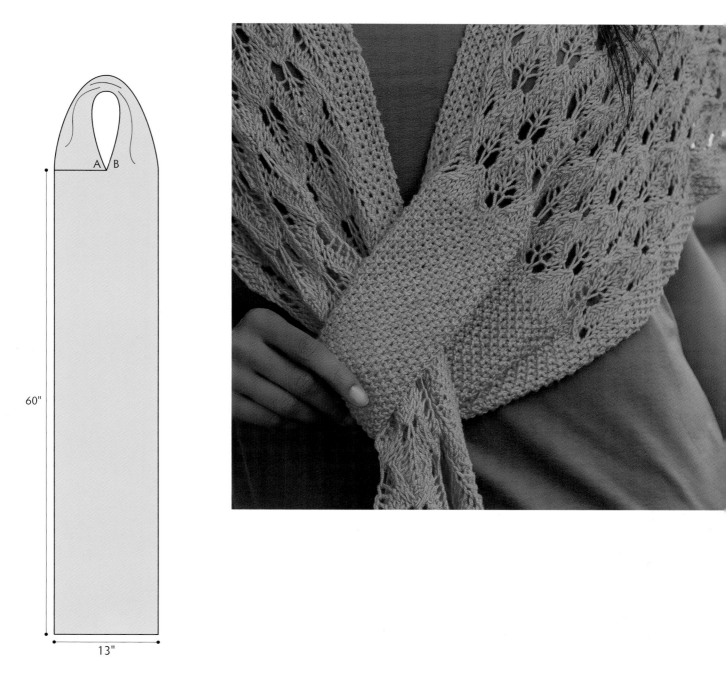

60"

13"

A B

Brussels Sprout

Finished Measurements: 43" at widest point x 28" x 15" at narrowest point excluding crochet edge

Brussels sprout: Cultivated for its small, leafy, dark-green buds that look like little cabbages on a tall stalk.

When worn loosely over your shoulders, this bobbled and cabled ribbed wrap with giant toggle button provides the right amount of warmth and an abundant amount of casual comfort. Show your support for a sometimes-underappreciated vegetable.

Materials

4 skeins of Tosh Vintage from Madelinetosh (100% superwash merino wool; 200 yds/182 m) in color Jade (4)

Size 10 (6 mm) needles or size required to obtain gauge

Cable needle

8 stitch markers

Size I-9 (5.5 mm) crochet hook

Tapestry needle

Toggle button, 6½ long

Gauge

16 sts = 4" in Brussels-sprout patt

Rib Pattern

(Over 7 sts)

Row 1 (RS): P2, K3, P2.

Row 2: K2, P3, P2.

Rep rows 1 and 2 for patt.

Brussels-Sprout Pattern

(Panel of 9 sts)

Note: This pattern is also charted; see page 21.

Row 1 (RS): Knit.

Row 2 and all even rows: Purl.

Row 3: C4B, K1, C4F.

Row 5: K4, MB, K4.

Row 7: K3, MB, K1, MB, K3.

Row 8: Purl.

Rep rows 1–8 for patt.

MB (make bobble): (K1, P1, K1, P1, K1) into next st, turn, P5, turn, pass sts 2, 3, 4, and 5, one at a time, over first st, knit this st tbl.

C4B: Sl 2 sts to cn, hold in back, K2, K2 from cn.

C4F: Sl 2 sts to cn, hold in front, K2, K2 from cn.

Wrap (Make 2 pieces.)

CO 61 sts.

Purl 1 row.

Setup row (RS): Work 3 St sts, pm, work 7 sts in row 1 of rib patt, pm, (work 9 sts in row 1 of Brussels-sprout patt, pm, work 7 rib sts, pm) 3 times, work 3 St sts.

Work in established patt until piece measures 28", ending with row 2.

BO all sts loosely.

Finishing

Place short side of 1 piece along edge of long side referring to schematic (page 21) and seam (see "Seaming Vertical Stitches to Horizontal Stitches" on page 75). With RS facing you and crochet hook, beg in 2nd st after any corner and make crocheted bobbles as follows.

MCB (MAKE CROCHET BOBBLE)

MCB: (Yarn around hook, draw up loop) 3 times in next st, draw up loop and pull through all 7 loops on hook.

Rnd 1: With RS facing you and crochet hook, sc along all edges, working 3 sc into each corner st. Join with sl st, ch 1.

Rnd 2: Work sc in same st as join, *MCB, ch 1, sk 1 st, rep from *, working MCB into each corner st and next st. Join with sl st and ch 1.

Rnd 3: Sc in each st, working 2 sc into each corner st. Fasten off, cut, and join with duplicate st.

Weave in ends. Block using mist-and-pin method (page 76) to smooth and even the sts.

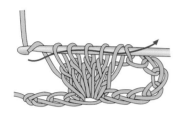

MAKE TOGGLE LOOP

With crochet hook, make 16" ch. Fasten off. Fold in half and attach center of ch in center of short side as for fringe (see "Applying Fringe" on page 76). Position toggle button and sew in place opposite chain. To fasten, wrap ends of ch around toggle button.

see "Applying Fringe" on page 76

Green Thumb Tip

Not a fan of Brussels sprouts—nor bobbles? Replace each bobble stitch with a knit stitch and you'll have a cabled and ribbed wrap, sans Brussels sprouts. If you can't locate a long toggle button, replace it with three smaller toggle buttons and crocheted loops.

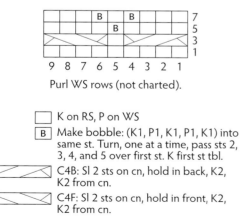

Purl WS rows (not charted).

☐ K on RS, P on WS

B Make bobble: (K1, P1, K1, P1, K1) into same st. Turn, one at a time, pass sts 2, 3, 4, and 5 over first st. K first st tbl.

C4B: Sl 2 sts on cn, hold in back, K2, K2 from cn.

C4F: Sl 2 sts on cn, hold in front, K2, K2 from cn.

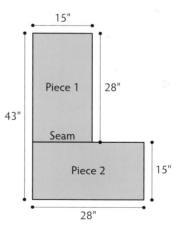

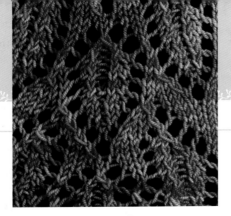

Clematis

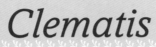

Finished Measurements: 6" x 76"

Clematis: Popular, hardy climbing vine with beautiful tropical-looking flowers.

A true perennial, this long clematis lace scarf will be a favorite, year after year. At first glance the pattern may look complicated, but don't be put off; as the clematis vine "grows" off your needles, you'll become familiar with the pattern and enjoy the knitting.

Materials

1 skein of Lace Merino from Ella Rae (100% extra-fine merino; 100 g; 480 yds/420 m) in color 120 Lilac, Denim, Rust **1**

Size 7 (4.5 mm) needles or size required to obtain gauge

2 stitch markers

Spare needle for holding stitches and binding off

Tapestry needle

Gauge

24 sts = 4" in clematis patt

Clematis Pattern

(Panel of 29 sts)

Note: This pattern is also charted; see page 25.

Row 1 (RS): K5, YO, K4, sk2p, YO, K2, P1, K2, YO, sk2p, K4, YO, K5.

Row 2: K1, (K1, P12) twice, K2.

Row 3: K3, K2tog, YO, K1, YO, K2tog tbl, K3, YO, K1, K2tog, P1, K2tog tbl, K1, YO, K3, K2tog, YO, K1, YO, K2tog tbl, K3.

Row 4: K2, P25, K2.

Row 5: K4, YO, K1, P1, K1, YO, sk2p, K1, YO, K1, K2tog, P1, K2tog tbl, K1, YO, K1, sk2p, YO, K1, P1, K1, YO, K4.

Row 6: K2, P4, K1, (P7, K1) twice, P4, K2.

Row 7: K4, YO, K2tog, P1, K2, YO, K2tog, YO, K1, K2tog, P1, K2tog tbl, K1, YO, K2tog, YO, K2, P1, K2tog tbl, YO, K4.

Row 8: K2, P4, K1, (P7, K1) twice, P4, K2.

Row 9: K4, YO, K2, P1, K2tog tbl, K1, YO, K2tog tbl, YO, K2tog, P1, K2tog tbl, YO, K2tog, YO, K1, K2tog, P1, K2, YO, K4.

Row 10: K2, P5, K1, (P6, K1) twice, P5, K2.

Row 11: K4, YO, K1, K2tog, P1, K2tog tbl, K1, YO, K2, YO, sk2p, YO, K2, YO, K1, K2tog, P1, K2tog tbl, K1, YO, K4.

Row 12: K2, P5, K1, P13, K1, P5, K2.

Row 13: K5, YO, K2tog, P1, K2tog tbl, K1, YO, K7, YO, K1, K2tog, P1, K2tog tbl, YO, K5.

Row 14: K2, P25, K2.

Row 15: K6, YO, (K2tog tbl) twice, K1, YO, K3, YO, K2tog tbl, K2, YO, K1, (K2tog) twice, YO, K6.

Row 16: K2, P25, K2.

Row 17: K7, YO, sk2p, YO, K2, K2tog, YO, K1, YO, K2tog tbl, K2, YO, sk2p, YO, K7.

Row 18: K2, P25, K2.

Row 19: K8, YO, K2tog tbl, K1, K2tog, YO, K1, P1, K1, YO, K2tog tbl, K1, K2tog, YO, K8.

Row 20: K1, (K1, P12) twice, K2.

Rep rows 1–20 for patt.

Scarf Half (Make 2)

CO 37 sts. Knit 2 rows.

Setup rows:

Row 1 (RS): K2, YO, K2tog, pm, K29 sts, pm, K4.

Row 2: K2, YO, K2tog, sl marker, P29, sl marker, K4.

Row 3: K2, YO, K2tog, sl marker, K14, YO, K2tog tbl, K13, sl marker, K4.

Row 4: K2, YO, K2tog, sl marker, K2, P25, K2, sl marker, K4.

Row 5: K2, YO, K2tog, K12, K2tog, YO, K1, YO, K2tog tbl, K12, K4.

Row 6: K2, YO, K2tog, sl marker, K2, P25, K2, sl marker, K4.

Row 7: K2, YO, K2tog, K11, K2tog, YO, K1, P1, K1, YO, K2tog tbl, K11, sl marker, K4.

Row 8: K2, YO, K2tog, sl marker, K1, (K1, P12) twice, K2, sl marker, K4.

Setup row (RS): K2, YO, K2tog, sl marker, work row 1 of clematis patt over 29 sts, sl marker, K4.

Cont in established patt, work first 4 sts as K2, YO, K2tog, sl marker, work 29 sts of patt, and ending sl marker, K4 until piece measures 38" slightly stretched, ending with row 20.

Knit 1 row.

Place sts on spare needle and set aside. Make second piece.

Finishing

With RS tog and WS facing out, join pieces using 3-needle BO (page 74). Weave in ends.

Wet block (page 76) to smooth and even the sts.

Green Thumb Tip

For an added embellishment, weave a narrow ribbon through the eyelets on each side of the scarf. Extra ribbon could also be applied as fringe across the bottom edges.

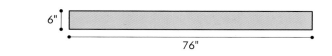

6" × 76"

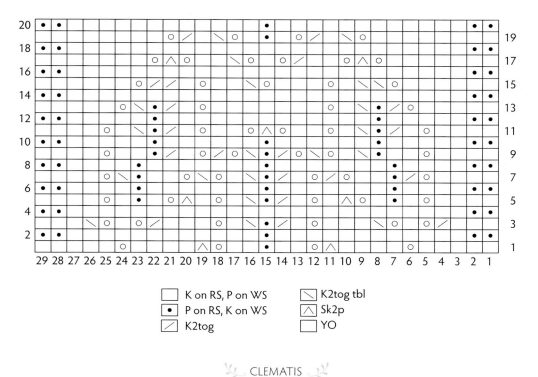

- ☐ K on RS, P on WS
- • P on RS, K on WS
- ╱ K2tog
- ╲ K2tog tbl
- ∧ Sk2p
- ☐ YO

Colorado Blue Spruce

Sizes: Small/Medium (Large/Extra Large)
Finished Measurements: 19½ (19½)" x 35 (40)"

Colorado blue spruce: A favored conifer with a distinctive pyramid shape. The dense, stiff branches with blue-green needles are often brought inside for ornamental and decorating purposes and are thought to promote good cheer.

This distinctive shrug with attractive styling, rolled-back ribbed edges, and a lace spruce-tree motif is a joy to work. It's quick and easy even though the written pattern is long. Definitely a pattern that will keep the knitter in good cheer.

Materials

4 (6) skeins of KidLin Light-Worsted Weight from Louet (53% kid mohair, 24% linen, 23% nylon; 50 g; 120 yds) in color 17 Colorado Spruce (●3)

Size 10½ (6.5 mm) needles or size required to obtain gauge

Size 11 (8 mm) needles or one size larger than needles required for gauge

Tapestry needle

Gauge

12 sts = 4" in Colorado-blue-spruce patt

Rib Edge Pattern

(Multiple of 5 + 2 sts)

Row 1 (RS): K2, *P3, K2, rep from * to end.

Row 2: Purl.

Rep rows 1 and 2 for patt.

Colorado-Blue-Spruce Pattern

(Multiple of 16 + 7 sts)

Note: This pattern is also charted; see page 29.

Row 1 (RS): K4, *K5, K2tog, YO, K1, YO, ssk, K6, rep from * to last 3 sts, K3.

Row 2 and all even rows: Purl.

Row 3: K4, *K4, K2tog, YO, K3, YO, ssk, K5, rep from * to last 3 sts, K3.

Row 5: K4, *K3, (K2tog, YO) twice, K1, (YO, ssk) twice, K4, rep from * to last 3 sts, K3.

Row 7: K4, *K2, (K2tog, YO) twice, K3, (YO, ssk) twice, K3, rep from * to last 3 sts, K3.

Row 9: K4, *K1, (K2tog, YO) 3 times, K1, (YO, ssk) 3 times, K2, rep from * to last 3 sts, K3.

Row 11: K4, *K2, (K2tog, YO) twice, K3, (YO, ssk) twice, K3, rep from * to last 3 sts, K3.

Row 13: K4, *K3, (K2tog, YO) twice, K1, (YO, ssk) twice, K4, rep from * to last 3 sts, K3.

Row 15: K4, *K4, K2tog, YO, K3, YO, ssk, K5, rep from * to last 3 sts, K3.

Row 17: K4, *K3, (K2tog, YO) twice, K1, (YO, ssk) twice, K4, rep from * to last 3 sts, K4.

Row 19: K4, *K2, (K2tog, YO) twice, K3, (YO, ssk) twice, K3, rep from * to last 3 sts, K3.

Row 21: K4, *K3, (K2tog, YO) twice, K1, (YO, ssk) twice, K4, rep from * to last 3 sts, K3.

Row 23: K4, *K4, K2tog, YO, K3, YO, ssk, K5, rep from * to last 3 sts, K3.

Row 25: K4, *K5, K2tog, YO, K1, YO, ssk, K6, rep from * to last 3 sts, K3.

Row 27: K4, *K6, K2tog, YO, K8, rep from * to last 3 sts, K3.

Row 29: K12, *K5, K2tog, YO, K1, YO, ssk, K6, rep from * to last 11 sts, K11.

Row 31: K12, *K4, K2tog, YO, K3, YO, ssk, K5, rep from * to last 11 sts, K11.

Row 33: K12, *K3, (K2tog, YO) twice, K1, (YO, ssk) twice, K4, rep from * to last 11 sts, K11.

Row 35: K12, *K2, (K2tog, YO) twice, K3, (YO, ssk) twice, K3, rep from * to last 11 sts, K11.

Row 37: K12, *K1, (K2tog, YO) 3 times, K1, (YO, ssk) 3 times, K2, rep from * to last 11 sts, K11.

Row 39: K12, *K2, (K2tog, YO) twice, K3, (YO, ssk) twice, K3, rep from * to last 10 sts, K11.

Row 41: K12, *K3, (K2tog, YO) twice, K1, (YO, ssk) twice, K4, rep from * to last 11 sts, K11.

Row 43: K12, * K4, K2tog, YO, K3, YO, ssk, K5, rep from * to last 11 sts, K11.

Row 45: K12, *K3, (K2tog, YO) twice, K1, (YO, ssk) twice, K4, rep from * to last 11 sts, K11.

Row 47: K12, *K2, (K2tog, YO) twice, K3, (YO, ssk) twice, K3, rep from * to last 11 sts, K11.

Row 49: K12, *K3, (K2tog, YO) twice, K1, (YO, ssk) twice, K4, rep from * to last 11 sts, K11.

Row 51: K12, *K4, K2tog, YO, K3, YO, ssk, K5, rep from * to last 11 sts, K11.

Row 53: K12, *K5, K2tog, YO, K1, YO, ssk, K6, rep from * to last 11 sts, K11.

Row 55: K12, *K6, K2tog, YO, K8, rep from * to last 11 sts, K11.

Row 56: Purl.

Work rows 1–56 for patt.

Shrug

With size 11 needles, CO 107 (122) sts.

Purl 1 row.

Work in rib edge patt until piece measures 5", ending with purl row.

Change to size 10½ needles.

Dec row (RS): (K20 [35], K2tog) 4 (3) times, K19 (11)—103 (119) sts.

Purl 1 row.

Work Colorado-blue-spruce patt until piece measures 33", ending with row 58.

Inc row (RS): (K20 [35], k1f&b) 4 (3) times, K19 (11)—107 (122) sts.

Purl 1 row.

Change to size 11 needles and work rib edge patt for 5", ending with purl row.

BO all sts loosely in patt.

Finishing

Fold piece in half so that BO and CO edges are tog. Measure 8" down from fold along each edge and mark for armhole. Seam side from bottom edge to mark (see "Mattress Stitch" on page 75). Weave in ends. Block using mist method (page 76) to smooth and even the sts.

Green Thumb Tip

Generally, smaller needles are used to work a ribbed edge, but in this project larger needles are used to give a looser, more desirable edge.

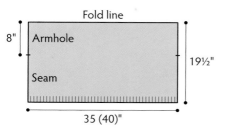

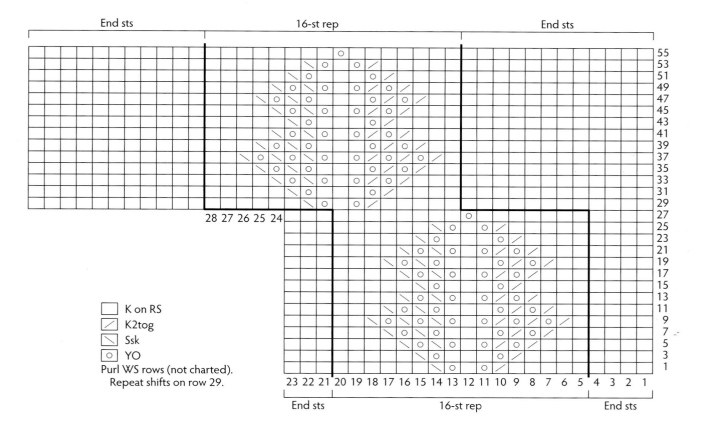

K on RS
K2tog
Ssk
YO
Purl WS rows (not charted).
Repeat shifts on row 29.

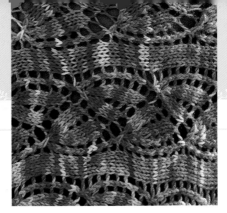

Daylily

Finished Measurements: 19" x 50"

Daylily: As the name implies, this attractive flower opens at sunrise and begins to wither at sunset, with another bud on the same stalk ready to undergo the same process the next day.

Reminiscent of an earlier age, this shrug with three-quarter-length sleeves, I-cord trim, and a lovely daylily lace pattern is worked in a rich colorway of merino, cashmere, and silk. This is a piece you will want to wear every day, all day long.

Materials

2 skeins of Richness of Martens Fingering from Alisha Goes Around (75% fine superwash merino wool, 15% cashmere, 10% silk; 115 g; 400 yds) in color Hot through October

Small amount of waste yarn of similar thickness

Size 8 (5 mm) needles or size required to obtain gauge

Size 8 double-pointed needles for I-cord

6 stitch markers

Tapestry needle

Gauge

21 sts = 4" in daylily patt

Daylily Pattern

(Multiple of 19 sts)

Note: Stitch count changes from row to row; count number of sts after rows 1, 9, or 15. This pattern is also charted; see page 33.

Row 1 (RS): *K2, YO, K2tog, YO, (K2tog) 3 times, K2, YO, K3, YO, ssk, YO, K2, rep from * to end.

Row 2: Purl.

Row 3: *K2, YO, K2tog, (K3tog) twice, YO, K1, YO, K2, (ssk, YO) twice, K2, rep from * to end—2 sts dec per rep.

Row 4: *P11, P2tog, P4, rep from * to end—1 st dec per rep.

Row 5: *K2, YO, K3tog, YO, K3, YO, K2, (ssk, YO) twice, K2, rep from * to end—1 st inc per rep.

Row 6: Purl.

Row 7: *K2, YO, K2tog, YO, K1, (YO, K2, ssk) twice, YO, ssk, YO, K2, rep from * to end—2 sts inc per rep.

Row 8: Purl.

Row 9: *K2, YO, K2tog, YO, K3, YO, K2, (ssk) 3 times, YO, ssk, YO, K2, rep from * to end.

Row 10: Purl.

Row 11: *K2, (YO, K2tog) twice, K2, YO, K1, YO, (sk2p) twice, ssk, YO, K2, rep from * to end—2 sts dec per rep.

Row 12: *P4, P2tog tbl, P11, rep from * to end—1 st dec per rep.

Row 13: *K2, (YO, K2tog) twice, K2, YO, K3, YO, sk2p, YO, K2, rep from * to end—1 st inc per rep.

Row 14: Purl.

Row 15: *K2, YO, K2tog, YO, (K2tog, K2, YO) twice, K1, YO, ssk, YO, K2, rep from * to end—2 sts inc per rep.

Row 16: Purl.

Rep rows 1–16 for patt.

Knit-In I-Cord Edge

(Worked over 3 sts at beg and 3 sts at end of row)

Row 1 (RS): K3, work as instructed to last 3 sts, sl 3 sts wyib.

Row 2: P3, work as instructed to last 3 sts, sl 3 sts wyif.

Rep rows 1 and 2 for patt.

Shrug

With waste yarn, CO 51 sts using provisional CO (page 73). Change to project yarn.

Purl 1 row.

Work 8 rows St st.

Inc row (RS): K1, M1, *K1, M1, rep from * to last st, end K1—101 sts.

Work 4 rows St st, beg with a purl row.

Setup row (WS): P3, pm, (P19, pm) 5 times, P3.

Work knit-in I-cord edge over first 3 sts, sl marker, (work 19-st daylily patt, sl marker) 5 times, end with 3 sts of knit-in I-cord edge.

Cont in established patt until piece measures 48" when slightly stretched, ending with row 16 of daylily patt. Remove all markers while working row 16.

Work 4 rows St st.

Dec row (RS): K1, K3tog, *K2tog, rep from * to last 5 sts, end K3tog, K2tog—50 sts.

Work 9 rows St st, beg with a purl row.

BO using applied I-cord as follows: K4, *sl 4 sts from right needle back to left needle, K3, ssk, rep from * until all sts have been used, 4 sts rem on right needle, pass 3 sts over last st, work and fasten off last st.

Remove waste yarn from CO edge, picking up sts. BO with applied cord.

Finishing

Block using wet blocking method (page 76) to smooth and even the sts. Create 2¼" cuff seam (see "Mattress Stitch" on page 75) between beg of knit-in I-cord and cuff-applied I-cord. Weave in ends.

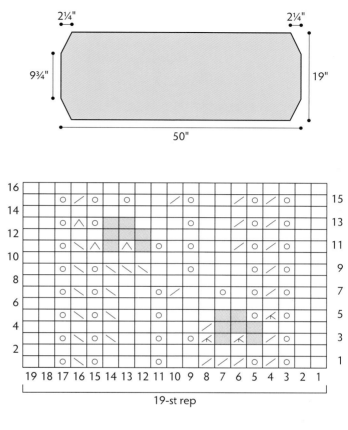

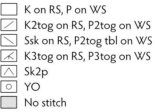

	K on RS, P on WS
/	K2tog on RS, P2tog on WS
\	Ssk on RS, P2tog tbl on WS
⋏	K3tog on RS, P3tog on WS
∧	Sk2p
o	YO
	No stitch

Hop Vines

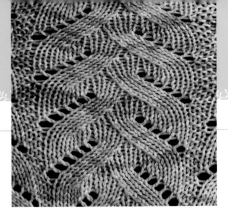

Hop vines: Fast-growing, climbing vines with large leaves that provide an ornamental screen. People familiar with hops know that it's what gives beer and ale their distinctive aroma, bitter taste, and old-world charm.

This modern shawl is complete with a vine-like climbing lace pattern and crocheted hops border. Wear it to a beer garden and strike up a knowledgeable conversation about hops.

Finished Measurements: 17" x 77"

Materials

2 skeins of Crock-O-Dye from Knit One, Crochet Too (65% superwash wool, 20% nylon, 15% silk; 100 g; 416 yds) in color 511 Sage (1)

Size 7 (4.5 mm) needles or size required to obtain gauge

Size 13 (9 mm) needle for binding off

Size 7 (4.5 mm) crochet hook

Tapestry needle

Gauge

16 sts = 4" in hop-vines patt

Hop-Vines Pattern

(Multiple of 18 + 2 sts, plus casting on 3 sts at beg of every row)

Note: Use cable cast on (page 73) to cast on at beg of each row. The sts cast on at the beg of the row are worked in St st. This pattern is also charted (shows repeat only); see page 36.

Row 1 (RS): CO 3 sts using cable CO method (here and throughout), K4 (first 3 sts are the newly CO sts, here and throughout), *P1, K3, YO, K2, ssk, K5, K2tog, K2, YO, P1, rep from *, end K1—23 sts.

Row 2 and all even rows: CO 3 sts, purl to end of row.

Row 3: CO 3 sts, K7, *P1, K4, YO, K2, ssk, K3, K2tog, K2, YO, K1, P1, rep from *, end K4.

Row 5: CO 3 sts, K10, *P1, K5, YO, K2, ssk, K1, K2tog, K2, YO, K2, P1, rep from *, end K7.

Row 7: CO 3 sts, K13, *P1, YO, K2, ssk, K5, K2tog, K2, YO, K3, P1, rep from *, end K10.

Row 9: CO 3 sts, K16, *P1, K1, YO, K2, ssk, K3, K2tog, K2, YO, K4, P1, rep from *, end K13.

Row 11: CO 3 sts, K19, *P1, K2, YO, K2, ssk, K1, K2tog, K2, YO, K5, P1, rep from *, end K16.

Row 12: CO 3 sts, purl to end of row.

Rep rows 1–12 for patt.

Shawl

Shawl is worked from bottom center point of triangle to top edge.

With size 7 needles, CO 20 sts. Purl 1 row.

Beg hop-vines patt and cont until piece measures approx 16½", ending with row 12—308 sts.

Work 4 rows St st.

With size 13 needle, BO all sts very loosely.

Finishing

With RS facing you and crochet hook, beg at corner of last BO st and work rnds 1–3 as described below.

Rnd 1: Sc along all edges, working 3 sc into each corner sts, join with sl st.

Rnd 2: Ch 6 (counts as dc and ch-3 space), dc in same st, *ch 3, skip next sc, dc in next sc, rep from * to corner at top edge; along top edge, sc in each sc.

Rnd 3: *In next ch-3 space, work (sc, ch 4, sc), rep from * around to corner at top edge; along top edge, sc in each sc.

Fasten off.

Weave in ends and block using mist-and-pin method (page 76) to smooth and even the sts.

(page 76)

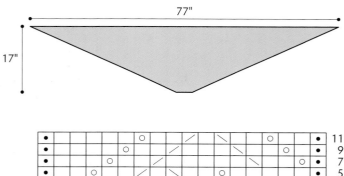

77"

17"

| 18 | 17 | 16 | 15 | 14 | 13 | 12 | 11 | 10 | 9 | 8 | 7 | 6 | 5 | 4 | 3 | 2 | 1 |

18-st rep

	Knit		Ssk
•	Purl	○	YO
/	K2tog		Purl WS rows (not charted).

Green Thumb Tip

One-skein project: A single-skein version of this pattern will give a smaller yet fashionable shawlette. Measure and wind 100 yards off the skein and set aside for the crochet trim. Work the shawl as directed until you're almost out of yarn. Bind off and finish as directed.

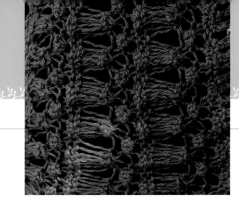

Hyacinth

Finished Measurements: 15½" x 52" excluding laced ribbon

Hyacinth: Sturdy upright stems support dense clusters of fragrant and fancy spring blooms.

Rows and rows of these astonishing fancy flowers are laced together with Hanah silk ribbon for a dramatic accent. This is the perfect wrap to wear on March 7—World Hyacinth Day!

Materials

4 skeins of Linsey from Berroco (64% cotton, 36% linen; 50 g; 114 yds) in color 6553 Hyacinth (**4**)

Size 10 (6 mm) needles or size required to obtain gauge

5 yds of ⁷⁄₁₆"-wide Hanah silk ribbon in color Abalone

2 safety pins

Tapestry needle

Gauge

18 sts = 4" in hyacinth patt

Hyacinth Pattern

(Multiple of 6 + 4 sts)

Note: This pattern is also charted; see page 39.

Row 1 (WS): K2, *sl 2, P3tog, p2sso, (K1, YO, K1, YO, K1) in same st, rep from * to last 2 sts, K2.

Rows 2 and 4: K2, purl to last 2 sts, K2.

Row 3: K2, *(K1, YO, K1, YO, K1) in same st, sl 2, P3tog, p2sso, rep from * to last 2 sts, K2.

Row 5: K2, *K1, wrapping yarn 3 times around needle, rep from * to last 2 sts, K2.

Row 6: K2, *purl, dropping extra wraps, rep from * to last 2 sts, K2. At end of row, gently pull knitting down from needle to lengthen sts.

Rep rows 1–6 for patt.

Shawl Half (Make 2.)

CO 70 sts. Knit 1 row.

Work in hyacinth patt until piece measures approx 26", ending with row 6.

Knit 2 rows.

Eyelet row (WS): K1, *K2tog, YO, rep from * to last st, K1.

Knit 1 row.

BO all sts loosely.

Rep for second piece.

LACING

Place both pieces of wrap on flat surface with RS facing you and BO edges approximately 2" apart. Place small safety pin in each end of ribbon to assist with lacing. Insert ribbon lace straight across the bottom, emerging from both bottom eyelets. Adjust so that both strands are the same length.

The left ribbon is worked up the left side and the right ribbon is worked up the right side. Loop each ribbon around the other in the center of the gap and thread the pin up through the next eyelet. Repeat until ribbon is threaded through all eyelets. Adjust ribbon as needed so width of gap is even. Weave ends of ribbon straight across top edge and weave in ends.

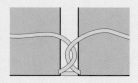

Finishing

Weave in ends. Block using mist method (page 76). Join by lacing with ribbon (see "Lacing" at left). Adjust width of lacing to your preference. Trim ends of ribbon as desired.

Green Thumb Tip

Use straight needles rather than circular ones to avoid the extra wraps rolling under themselves and getting caught when moving between cable and needle.

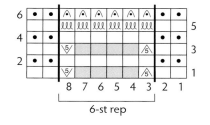

	K on RS, P on WS
•	P on RS, K on WS
/5\	Sl 2, P3tog, P2sso
5/	(K1, YO, K1, YO, K1) in same st
⊍⊍⊍	K1 wrapping 3 times
∧	P, dropping extra wraps
	No stitch

6-st rep

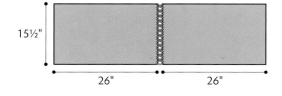

15½"

26"   26"

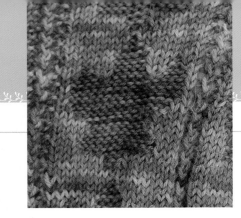

Maple Leaf

Finished Measurements: 20" x 58"

Materials

4 skeins of Alpaca Blend from Mountain Colors (50% alpaca, 50% wool; 75 g; 150 yds) in color Yellowstone (4)

Size 8 (5 mm) needles or size required to obtain gauge

Extra size 8 (5 mm) needle for binding off

Small amount of waste yarn

6 stitch markers

Tapestry needle

Gauge

18 sts = 4" in St st

Rickrack Pattern

(Multiple of 3 + 1 sts)

Row 1 (RS): K1, *YO, ssk, K1, rep from * to end.

Row 2: K1, *YO, P2tog, K1, rep from * to end.

Rep rows 1 and 2 for patt.

Maple-Leaf Pattern

(Panel of 17 sts)

Note: This pattern is also charted; see page 42.

Maple leaf: The leaves of the popular maple tree spurred the long-standing practice of fall-tourism: traveling to see leaves turn a gorgeous array of spectacular gold, orange, yellow, and red hues.

Surround yourself in autumnal beauty with this reversible Möbius wrap with embossed maple leaf and rickrack lace trim.

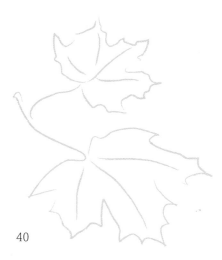

Row 1 (RS): K7, P3, K7.

Row 2: P7, K3, P7.

Row 3: K3, P11, K3.

Row 4: P3, K11, P3.

Row 5: K4, P9, K4.

Row 6: P5, K7, P5.

Row 7: K4, P9, K4.

Row 8: P2, K13, P2.

Row 9: K2, P13, K2.

Row 10: P1, K15, P1.

Row 11: K1, P15, K1.

Row 12: P1, K15, P1.

Row 13: K1, P4, K1, P5, K1, P4, K1.

Row 14: P2, K2, P2, K5, P2, K2, P2.

Row 15: K2, P1, K3, P5, K3, P1, K2.

Row 16: P6, K5, P6.

Row 17: K7, P3, K7.

Row 18: P8, K1, P8.

Row 19: K8, P1, K8.

Row 20: P17.

Rep rows 1–20 for patt.

Wrap

With waste yarn, CO 79 sts using provisional CO (page 73).

Purl 1 row.

Setup row (RS): Work 10 sts in row 1 of rickrack patt, pm, (work 17 sts in row 1 of maple-leaf patt, pm, work 4 sts in rickrack patt, pm) twice, work 17 sts in maple-leaf patt, pm, work 10 sts in rickrack patt.

Cont in established patt until piece measures 58", ending with row 20 of maple-leaf patt.

Knit 1 row. Leave sts on needle.

Finishing

With sts still on needle, block using mist-and-pin method (page 76) to smooth and even the sts. Remove waste yarn from CO edge, with extra needle, PU 79 sts. Create Möbius strip by bringing needles tog and twisting one end 180° before working 3-needle BO. Weave in ends. Lightly mist BO edge if desired.

Green Thumb Tip

To make a traditional rectangular wrap, using long-tail cast on, work as directed and BO normally. Do not seam. With size H-8 (5 mm) crochet hook, sc along CO and BO edges.

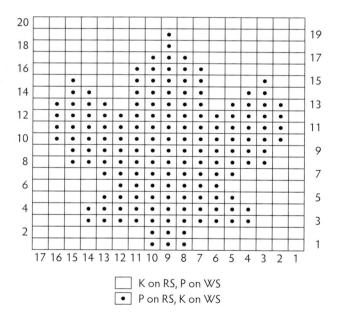

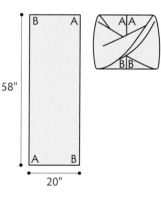

K on RS, P on WS
• P on RS, K on WS

Ornamental Corn

Finished Measurements: 18" x 66"

Ornamental corn: Beautiful multicolored rows of corn kernels turn darker as the cob dries, making this corn a fall favorite for decorative crafts and ornamental arrangements.

This stitch pattern creates beautiful rows of "corn kernels," and the dense, thick fabric is soft and comfy. Stay warm in this casual wrap, styled with one buttonhole and two buttons for several wearing options.

Materials

Baby Alpaca Grande Hand Dye from Plymouth Yarn Company (100% baby alpaca; 100 g; 110 yds) (5)

> **A:** 4 skeins in color 6 Brown Multi
>
> **B:** 4 skeins in color 14 Blue Multi
>
> **C:** 1 skein in color 4 Orange Multi

Size 17 (12 mm) needles or size required to obtain gauge

Size J-10 (6 mm) crochet hook

2 buttons, 1¾" diameter

2 buttons in slightly smaller size

Tapestry needle

Gauge

12 sts = 4" in corn patt

Corn Pattern

(Even number of sts)

Row 1 (RS): With B, K1, *K1, sl 1 wyib, rep from * to last st, K1.

Row 2: With B, K1, *sl 1 wyif, K1, rep from * to last st, K1.

Row 3: With A, K1, *sl 1 wyib, K1tbl, rep from * to last st, K1.

Row 4: With A, K1, *K1, sl 1 wyif, rep from * to last st, K1.

Rep rows 1–4 for patt.

Wrap

With A, CO 54 sts and knit 1 row.

Beg corn patt and cont until piece measures 11", ending with row 2.

Buttonhole row (RS): Work 12 sts in patt, K2tog, sl last st worked to LH needle, K2tog, cont in corn patt as established across row.

Next row: Work in patt to last 12 sts. Using backward loop, CO 2 sts, cont in corn patt across row. Cont in patt until piece measures 66", ending with row 2.

With A, knit 1 row, BO pw all sts loosely.

Finishing

With RS facing you and using crochet hook and C, sc along all edges, working 3 sc into each corner st. Mark placement for first button on opposite end from buttonhole, 11" from short side and 4" from neck edge. Position second button 10" up from first button. Sew buttons and backs in

BACKING BUTTONS

Since the decorative buttons I used are flat (they don't have shanks), attaching a back button to each helps stabilize the front button and provides the extra space needed for buttoning a bulky knit. The back button can be plain and smaller than the front button, but must have the same number of holes. To sew in place, position the decorative button on the right side of knit fabric and the back button on the wrong side, with holes aligned. Place a spacer, such as a spare tapestry needle or thin cable needle, between the front button and knit fabric, making sure not to obstruct the holes in the buttons. Sew both buttons together through the knit fabric securely with matching yarn. Remove the spacer.

place, referring to "Backing Buttons" (left). Weave in ends and block using mist method (page 76) to smooth and even the sts.

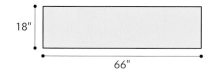

18"

66"

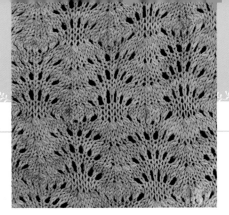

Ostrich-Plume Fern

Finished Measurements: Approx 20" x 72"

Ostrich-plume fern: A classic fern with graceful soft fronds.

This is a timeless shawl with delicate curvy edges and high-lighted with a bit of silver floss spun into the yarn.

Materials

2 skeins of Starry from Dream In Color Yarn (98% Australian merino wool, 2% silver floss; 4 oz; 450 yds) in color 140 Spring Tickle (**1**)

Size 7 (4.5 mm) needles or size required to obtain gauge

2 stitch markers

Tapestry needle

Shawl pin (optional)

Gauge

20 sts = 4" in ostrich-plume-fern patt

Ostrich-Plume-Fern Pattern

(Multiple of 16 + 1 sts)

Note: This pattern is also charted; see page 48.

Rows 1, 5, 9, 13, 17, 21, 25, and 29 (RS): Knit.

Row 2 and all even rows: Purl.

Rows 3, 7, 11, and 15: (K1, YO) 3 times, *(ssk) twice, s2kp, (K2tog) twice, (YO, K1) 5 times, YO, rep from *, end (ssk) twice, s2kp, (K2tog) twice, (YO, K1) 3 times.

Rows 19, 23, 27, and 31: (K2tog) 3 times, *(YO, K1) 5 times, YO, (ssk) twice, s2kp, (K2tog) twice, rep from *, end (YO, K1) 5 times, YO, (ssk) 3 times.

Row 32: Purl.

Rep rows 1–32 for patt.

Shawl

Cast on 101 sts.

Knit 2 rows.

Setup row (RS): K2, pm, work row 1 of ostrich-plume-fern patt to last 2 sts, pm, K2.

Cont in established patt, working first and last 2 sts in garter st until piece measures 70", ending with row 32.

Purl 1 row.

BO all sts pw.

Finishing

Weave in ends. Block using wet blocking method (page 76) to smooth and even the sts.

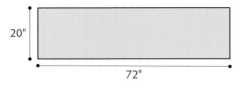

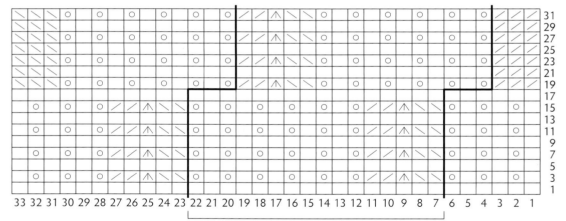

16-st rep

	Knit
╱	K2tog
╲	Ssk
⋀	S2kp
○	YO

Purl WS rows (not charted).

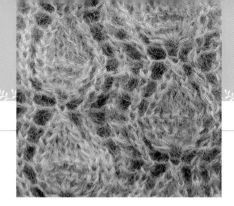

Pears

Finished Measurements: 5" x 40"

Pears: Deliciously sweet, delightfully crunchy, and beautifully golden.

This elegant ascot with golden pears suspended on a lacy trellis fits snugly around the neck. Slipping one end through the ribbed opening ensures the ascot will stay in place.

Materials

1 skein of Luna from S. Charles Collezione (71% super kid mohair, 20% silk, 9% lurex; 25 g; 232 yds) in color 26 Sunbeam (3)

Size 9 (5.5 mm) needles or size required to obtain gauge

Tapestry needle

Gauge

19 sts = 4" in pear patt with 2 strands of yarn held tog

Pear Pattern

(Multiple of 23 sts)

Note: This pattern is also charted; see page 51.

Row 1 (RS): Ssk, (YO, ssk) twice, K3, (K2tog, YO) twice, s2kp, YO, ssk, YO, (K1, YO, K1, YO, K1, YO, K1) in same st, (YO, K2tog) twice—27 sts.

Row 2 and all even rows: Purl.

Row 3: Ssk, (YO, ssk) twice, K1, (K2tog, YO) twice, s2kp, YO, ssk, YO, K1, P5, K1, (YO, K2tog) twice—25 sts.

Row 5: (Ssk, YO) twice, s2kp, YO, K2tog, YO, s2kp, YO, ssk, YO, K1, P5, K1, (YO, K2tog) twice—23 sts.

Row 7: (Ssk, YO) twice, (K1, YO, K1, YO, K1, YO, K1) in same st, YO, K2tog, YO, s2kp, (YO, ssk) twice, K3, (K2tog, YO) twice, K2tog—27 sts.

Row 9: (Ssk, YO) twice, K1, P5, K1, YO, K2tog, YO, s2kp, (YO, ssk) twice, K1, (K2tog, YO) twice, K2tog—25 sts.

Row 11: (Ssk, YO) twice, K1, P5, K1, YO, K2tog, YO, s2kp, YO, ssk, YO, sk2p, (YO, K2tog) twice—23 sts.

Row 12: Purl.

Rep rows 1–12 for patt.

Ascot

Bottom edge:

With 2 strands of yarn held tog, CO 11.

Knit 2 rows.

Next row: K1f&b into each st—22 sts.

Next row (RS): K1, K1f&b, knit to end of row—23 sts.

Purl 1 row.

Work in pear patt until piece measures approx 8½", ending with row 12.

Ribbed opening:

Next row (RS): K1, K2tog, knit to end of row—22 sts.

Place every other st on holder, leaving rem sts on needle.

With sts rem on needle (half of total number), work in K1, P1 rib for 2¼", place on holder and cut yarn, leaving 4" tail. Place sts from first holder back onto needle and work in K1, P1 rib for 2¼", ending with WS row. Leave sts on needle.

Next row (RS): With RS facing you, knit, alternating 1 st from holder and 1 st from needle to rejoin halves—22 sts.

Next row: P1, P1f&b, purl to end of row—23 sts.

Neck piece:

Resume pear patt and work even until piece measures approx 16" from ribbing, ending with row 12.

Ribbed slip through:

Next row (RS): K1, K2tog, knit to end of row—22 sts.

Next row: P2tog to end of row—11 sts.

Work in K1, P1 rib for 2¼", ending with WS row.

Next row (RS): K1f&b in all sts—22 sts.

Next row: P1, P1f&b, purl to end of row—23 sts.

Bottom edge:

Work in pear patt until piece measures 8½", ending with row 12.

Next row (RS): K1, K2tog, knit to end of row—22 sts.

Next row: K2tog to end of row—11 sts.

Knit 2 rows.

BO all sts loosely.

Finishing

Weave in ends. Block using mist-and-pin method (page 76) to smooth and even the sts.

Green Thumb Tip

To work using two strands of yarn from one ball, pull one strand from the center and the other from the outside. Place the ball in a bowl to prevent it from rolling around.

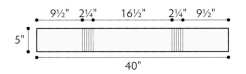

9½"   2¼"   16½"   2¼"   9½"

5"

40"

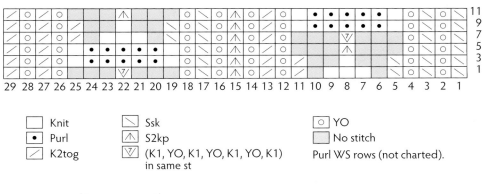

	Knit		Ssk		YO
•	Purl	⟋	S2kp		No stitch
⟋	K2tog		(K1, YO, K1, YO, K1, YO, K1) in same st		Purl WS rows (not charted).

Red Beets

Finished Measurements: Circumference: 34" Height: 19"

Beets: Deep, rich red to purple root vegetable that's low in calories, deliciously high in nutritional value, and is a work of art—when sliced, its insides reveal beautiful concentric circles.

Worked in the round, this cowl, with easy rolled edges and artistic concentric lace circles, is a must-have winter accessory. Wear it instead of a scarf, as a hat, or over a crew neckline as a cowl.

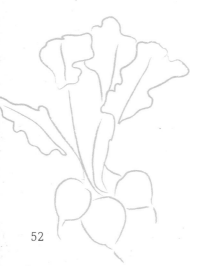

Materials

2 skeins of Shepherd Worsted from Lorna's Laces (100% superwash wool; 4 oz; 225 yds) in color 205 Irving Park

Size 10 (6 mm) circular needle (24") or size required to obtain gauge

Size 11 (8 mm) needle for binding off

7 matching stitch markers

1 contrasting stitch marker

Tapestry needle

Gauge

14 sts = 4" in St st

Garter-Rib Pattern

(Multiple of 6 sts)

Rnd 1 (RS): Knit.

Rnd 2: K3, P3.

Rep rnds 1 and 2 for patt.

Beet Pattern

(Panel of 15 sts, worked in the round)

Note: This pattern is also charted; see page 55.

Rnd 1: K6, cluster 3, K6.

Rnd 2 and all even rnds: Knit.

Rnd 3: K4, K3tog, YO, K1fbf, YO, K3tog tbl, K4.

Rnd 5: K2, K3tog, YO, K2tog, YO, K1fbf, YO, K2tog tbl, YO, K3tog tbl, K2.

Rnd 7: K1, (K2tog, YO) 3 times, K1 tbl, (YO, K2tog tbl) 3 times, K1.

Rnd 9: K2, YO, (K2tog, YO) 2 times, sk2p, YO, (K2tog tbl, YO) twice, K2.

Rnd 11: K1, (K2tog tbl, YO) 3 times, K1 tbl, (YO, K2tog) 3 times, K1.

Rnd 13: K2, K1f&b, YO, K2tog tbl, YO, dec 5, YO, K2tog, YO, K1f&b, K2.

Rnd 15: K4, K1f&b, YO, dec 5, YO, K1f&b, K4.

Rnd 16: Knit.

Rep rnds 1–16 for patt.

Cluster 3: Sl 3 wyib, move yarn to front, sl same 3 sts to left needle, pass yarn to back, K3 (knit each of the 3 sts slipped).

Dec 5: K2tog tbl, K3tog, pass st from K2tog tbl over st of K3tog (4 sts decreased).

Cowl

With size 10 needle, CO 120 sts, pm to mark beg of rnd and join, being careful not to twist sts. Knit 6 rnds.

Work 4 rnds in garter-rib patt.

Knit 1 rnd.

Setup rnd: (K15, pm) 7 times, K15.

Work 16 rnds as follows: (Work 15 sts in beet patt, sl marker, K15, sl marker) 4 times.

Knit 1 rnd.

Work 4 rnds in garter-rib patt.

Knit 1 rnd.

Work 16 rnds as follows: (K15, sl marker, work 15 sts in beet patt, sl marker) 4 times.

Knit 1 rnd.

Work 4 rnds in garter-rib patt.

Knit 1 rnd.

Work 16 rnds as follows: (Work 15 sts in beet patt, sl marker, K15, sl marker) 4 times.

Work 16 rnds as follows: (K15, sl marker, work 15 sts in beet patt, sl marker) 4 times.

Knit 1 rnd.

Work 4 rnds in garter-rib patt.

Knit 1 rnd.

Work 16 rnds as follows: (K15, sl marker, work 15 sts in beet patt, sl marker) 4 times.

Knit 1 rnd.

Work 4 rnds in garter-rib patt.

Knit 1 rnd, removing markers, except for marker at beg of rnd.

Work 4 rnds in garter-rib patt.

Knit 7 rnds.

With size 11 needle, BO all sts loosely.

Finishing

Weave in ends. Block using mist method (page 76) to smooth and even the sts.

(page 76)

Green Thumb Tip

Consider making a shorter version, about 10" long, to be worn as a neck gaiter. Work as directed, working only two repeats of beet pattern.

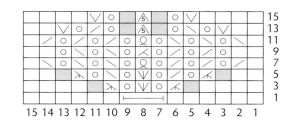

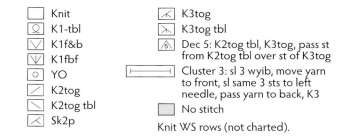

☐ Knit	⟋⟍	K3tog
Ⓠ K1-tbl	⟍⟋	K3tog tbl
⋁ K1f&b	⌇	Dec 5: K2tog tbl, K3tog, pass st from K2tog tbl over st of K3tog
⋁ K1fbf		
○ YO	⊢⊣	Cluster 3: sl 3 wyib, move yarn to front, sl same 3 sts to left needle, pass yarn to back, K3
⟋ K2tog		
⟍ K2tog tbl	▨	No stitch
⟍⟋ Sk2p		

Knit WS rows (not charted).

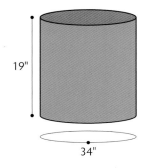

19"

34"

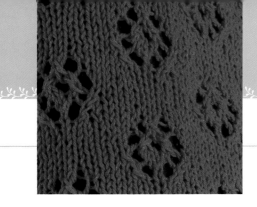

Roses

Finished Size: Neck edge: 30" excluding tab
Bottom edge: 44" excluding ruffle, Length: 17"

Roses: Prickly shrubs that bear lush, fragrant flowers. Roses have a long and colorful history as symbols of love, war, and beauty.

Be sure to stop and smell the roses while wearing this sassy wrap with ruffle, rose-lace pattern, and tab button closure.

Materials

5 skeins of Hempathy from Elsebeth Lavold (34% hemp, 41% cotton, 25% modal; 50 g; 140 m/153 yds) in color 30 Berlin Red ⓐ

Size 6 (4 mm) circular needle (29") or size required to obtain gauge

Size 8 (5 mm) needles for binding off or two sizes larger than gauge needle

2 stitch markers

Additional stitch markers for casting on (optional)

1 button, 1⅛" diameter

Tapestry needle

Gauge

18 sts = 4" in rosebud patt using size 6 needle

Ruffle Pattern

Rows 1 (RS)–4: Knit.

Rows 5–8: Purl.

Rows 9 and 11: Knit.

Rows 10 and 12: Purl.

Row 13: (K3tog) across row.

Row 14: Purl.

Row 15: Knit.

Beaded-Rib Pattern

(Multiple of 6 sts)

Row 1 (RS): *K3, P3, rep from * to end.

Row 2: *K1, P1, rep from * to end.

Rep rows 1 and 2 for patt.

Rosebud Pattern

(Multiple of 16 + 9 sts)

Row 1 (RS): K10, *K2tog, YO, K1, YO, ssk, K11, rep from * to last 15 sts, end K2tog, YO, K1, YO, ssk, K10.

Row 2 and all even rows: Purl.

Row 3: K9, *K2tog, YO, K3, YO, ssk, K9, rep from * to end.

Row 5: K10, *YO, ssk, YO, K3tog, YO, K11, rep from * to last 15 sts, end YO, ssk, YO, K3tog, YO, K10.

Row 7: K11, *YO, K3tog, YO, K13, rep from * to last 15 sts, end YO, K3tog, YO, K11.

Row 9: K2, *K2tog, YO, K1, YO, ssk, K11, rep from * to last 7 sts, end K2tog, YO, K1, YO, ssk, K2.

Row 11: K1, *K2tog, YO, K3, YO, ssk, K9, rep from * to last 8 sts, K2tog, YO, K3, YO, ssk, K1.

Row 13: K2, *YO, ssk, YO, K3tog, YO, K11, rep from * to last 7 sts, end YO, ssk, YO, K3tog, YO, K2.

Row 15: K3, *YO, K3tog, YO, K13, rep from * to last 6 sts, end YO, K3tog, YO, K3.

Row 16: Purl.

Rep rows 1–16 for patt.

Wrap

With size 8 needle, CO 591 sts.

Work 15 rows of ruffle patt—197 sts. Change to size 6 needle.

Setup row (WS): P6, pm, purl to last 6 sts, pm, P6.

Next row (RS): Work first 6 sts in beaded-rib patt, sl marker and work rosebud patt to next marker, sl marker, work last 6 sts in beaded-rib patt. Cont in established patt until piece measures 15", ending with row 16 of rosebud patt.

Work 2 rows St st, maintaining established beaded-rib patt for first 6 and last 6 sts.

Dec row (RS): Work 6 sts in beaded-rib patt, sl marker, K4, *K1, K2tog, rep

from * to 4 sts before marker, K4, sl marker, work 6 sts in beaded rib—138 sts.

Next row: Work 6 sts in beaded-rib patt, remove marker, purl to marker and remove, work 6 sts in beaded-rib patt.

Create buttonhole tab: CO 12 sts using backward-loop method (page 73).

Work 6 rows of beaded-rib patt.

Buttonhole row: K3, P2tog, sl st just made back to LH needle, K2tog, sl st just made to LH needle and K2tog, cont in beaded-rib patt.

Next row: Work in patt to last 3 sts, CO 3 sts using cable CO (page 73), work last 3 sts in patt.

Work 4 rows in beaded-rib patt.

With size 8 needle, BO loosely in patt.

Finishing

Weave in ends. Block using mist method (page 76). Determine button placement, about 2" in from side edge, adjusting for personal fit, and sew in place.

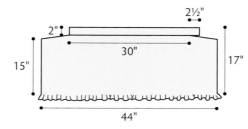

Tulips

Finished Measurements: 8" x 52"

Materials

2 skeins of Voile de la Mer from Tilli Tomas (70% silk, 30% seacell; 50 g; 290 yds) in color Coral Sap (2)

5½ yds of ⅝"-wide Hanah silk ribbon in color Monet

Size H-8 (5 mm) needles or size required to obtain gauge

Size G-6 (4 mm) crochet hook

Tapestry needle

Gauge

17 sts = 4" in patt (exact gauge is not critical)

Tulip Triangle Pattern

(Over 49 sts)

Rows 1–4: Knit.

Row 5: K24, P1, K24.

Row 6 (RS): K1, K2tog tbl, K19, K2tog, YO, K1, YO, K2tog tbl, K19, K2tog, K1—47 sts.

Row 7: K21, P5, K21.

Row 8: K20, K2tog, YO, K3, YO, K2tog tbl, K20.

Row 9: K20, P7, K20.

Row 10: K1, K2tog tbl, K16, (K2tog, YO) twice, K1, (YO, K2tog tbl) twice, K16, K2tog, K1—45 sts.

Row 11: K18, P9, K18.

Row 12: K17, (K2tog, YO) twice, K3, (YO, K2tog tbl) twice, K17.

Row 13: K17, P4, K1, P1, K1, P4, K17.

Row 14: K1, K2tog tbl, K13, P4, K2, P1, K2, P4, K13, K2tog, K1—43 sts.

Row 15: K15, P4, K2, P1, K2, P4, K15.

Row 16: K13, (K2tog, YO) twice, K3, YO, K1, YO, K3 (YO, K2tog tbl) twice, K13.

Row 17: K13, P4, K3, P3, K3, P4, K13.

Row 18: K1, K2tog tbl, K3, YO, K2tog tbl, K4, (K2tog, YO) twice, K4, YO, K1, YO, K4, (YO, K2tog tbl) twice, K4, K2tog, YO, K3, K2tog, K1—41 sts.

Row 19: K5, P2, K4, P4, K4, P3, K4, P4, K4, P2, K5.

Row 20: K6, YO, K2tog tbl, K3, (K2tog, YO) twice, K7, YO, K1, YO, K7, (YO, K2tog tbl) twice, K3, K2tog, YO, K6—47 sts.

Row 21: K6, P2, K3, P4, K5, P7, K5, P4, K3, P2, K6.

Tulips: Spring-blooming perennials cultivated for their beautiful, distinctive cup-shaped flowers, which are a favorite for fresh-cut bouquets.

Just as fresh-cut tulips drape over the sides of a vase, this distinctive accessory has exquisite drape. The garter-stitch, modular construction has a tulip budding in the center of each triangle and silk fringe at each intersection of triangles.

Row 22: K1, K2tog tbl, K4, YO, K2tog tbl, K1, (K2tog, YO) twice, K9, YO, K1, YO, K9, (YO, K2tog tbl) twice, K1, K2tog, YO, K4, K2tog, K1.

Row 23: K6, P2, K1, P4, K6, P9, K6, P4, K1, P2, K6.

Row 24: K7, YO, sk2p, YO, K2tog, YO, K7, K2tog tbl, K5, K2tog, K7, YO, K2tog tbl, YO, K3tog, YO, K7—45 sts.

Row 25: K7, P5, K7, P7, K7, P5, K7.

Row 26: K1, K2tog tbl, K16, K2tog tbl, K3, K2tog, K16, K2tog, K1—41 sts.

Row 27: K18, P5, K18.

Row 28: K18, K2tog tbl, K1, K2tog, K18—39 sts.

Row 29: K18, P3, K18.

Row 30: K1, K2tog tbl, K15, sk2p, K15, K2tog, K1—35 sts.

Rows 31–33: K35.

Row 34: K1, K2tog tbl, knit to last 3 sts, end K2tog, K1—33 sts.

Rows 35–37: Knit.

Rows 38–93: Rep rows 34–37 a total of 14 times until 5 sts rem.

Row 94: K1, sk2p, K1—3 sts.

Rows 95 and 96: Knit.

Row 97: Sk2p—1 st. After first, third, and fifth triangles are complete, do not cut yarn; with loop on needle, beg new triangle. After second, fourth, and sixth triangles are complete, fasten off and cut yarn before beg next triangle.

Scarf

For first triangle, CO 49 sts. Work tulip triangle patt. Do not cut yarn at end of triangle.

For triangle 2 and all even-numbered triangles, with 1 st on needle (last st from previous triangle), PU 48 sts with RS facing you—49 sts. Work tulip triangle patt, fasten off last st.

For odd-numbered triangles, PU 49 sts, see schematic for direction of work. Work a total of 6 triangles.

Finishing

Weave in all ends. With crochet hook and RS facing you, sc along entire edge, working 5 sc into each point. Block using mist method (page 76) to smooth and even the sts. Cut 16 strands of ribbon, each 12" long. With crochet hook and 2 strands held tog, fold fringe in half. Attach fringe at each intersection of triangles (see "Applying Fringe" on page 76).

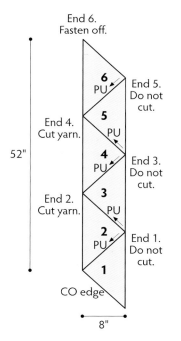

Violets

Finished Measurements: 40" x 40"

Violets: Solitary spring-blooming flowers vary in a strong violet color. Valued by ancient Greeks for their medicinal properties and for making wine, violets are used by modern chefs to decorate salads and crystallize for candy.

Wearing this decorative square shawl with a violet-pattern center and lace outer edging tipped with a beaded edge adds a lovely touch to any outfit.

Materials

2 skeins of Sock from Malabrigo Yarn (superwash merino wool; 3.5 oz; 440 yds) in color 808 Violeta Africana (**2**)

Size 7 (4.5 mm) circular needle (47") or size required to obtain gauge

8 ring markers (1 of one color, 7 of a different color)

Size 12 (1 mm) steel crochet hook or size small enough to fit through bead

508 size 6/0 beads in color Tanzanite

Tapestry needle

Gauge

21 sts and 28 rows = 4" in St st

Violet Pattern

(Multiple of 9 + 6 sts)

Note: This pattern is also charted; see page 64.

Row 1 (RS): K3, *K2, YO, ssk, K5, rep from * to last 3 sts, K3.

Row 2 and all even rows: Purl.

Row 3: K3, *K2tog, YO, K1, YO, ssk, K4, rep from * to last 3 sts, K3.

Rows 5 and 7: Knit.

Row 9: K3, *K6, YO, ssk, K1, rep from * to last 3 sts, K3.

Row 11: K3, *K4, K2tog, YO, K1, YO, ssk, rep from * to last 3 sts, K3.

Rows 13 and 15: Knit.

Row 16: Purl.

Rep rows 1–16 for patt.

Lace Edge Pattern

(Even number of sts in the round)

Rnd 1 (RS): (YO, K1, *YO, K2tog, rep from * to marker, YO, sl marker, K1, sl marker) 4 times—8 sts inc.

Rnd 2 and all even rnds: Knit.

Rnd 3: (YO, *ssk, YO, rep from * to 1 st before marker, K1, YO, sl marker, K1, sl marker) 4 times—8 sts inc.

Rnd 5: (YO, knit to marker, YO, sl marker, K1, sl marker) 4 times—8 sts inc.

Row 6: Knit.

Rep rows 1–6 for patt.

Shawl

CO 105 sts.

Work 4 rows St st.

Work rows 1–16 of violet patt 8 times, then work rows 1–8 once more.

BEADED BIND OFF

Check to be sure the head of the crochet hook fits through the bead. Purchase extra beads; some may need to be discarded due to a defective opening and some may prefer to hide in the couch or roll on the floor and never be seen again!

The beaded BO is worked like the standard bind off except that a bead is placed on each stitch.

Place bead: Slip bead on crochet hook, remove st just worked and place on hook, pull st through bead. Replace st on right needle.

1. Knit 1 st, place bead.

2. Knit 1 st, place bead.

3. Pass first st worked over last st worked as for standard bind off.

Rep steps 2 and 3 to complete bind off. Fasten off last st after placing bead.

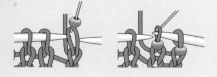

BO all sts loosely but do NOT fasten off final loop.

With RS facing you and last loop on needle, pm, PU 1 st in corner, pm, PU 105 sts along side edge, pm, PU 1 st in corner, pm, PU 105 sts along BO edge, pm, PU 1 st in corner, pm, PU 105 sts along side edge, pm, PU 1 st in corner, pm, PU 104 sts along CO edge, knit loop from BO. Pm of different color to mark end of rnd—424 sts.

Knit 1 rnd.

Work rows 1–6 of lace edge patt 7 times—592 sts.

BO all sts using beaded BO method (left).

Finishing

Weave in ends. Block using wet blocking method (page 76) or use blocking wires if available. If I'm blocking a rectangular stole, I start with one short end, and then run wires or line down the long edges and stretch lengthwise and widthwise, keeping the proportion true. I end with the second short

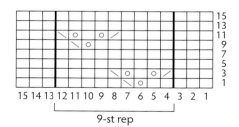

9-st rep

side. After the first "stretch," I get a tape measure and make sure that measurements of all sides or edges match. Keep adjusting until everything measures up. Let dry.

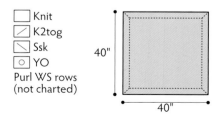

Knit
K2tog
Ssk
YO
Purl WS rows
(not charted)

40"

40"

Willow

Sizes: Small/Medium (Large/Extra Large)
Finished Measurements: Bottom edge: 54 (62)"
Neck edge: 18 (18)", Length: 16 (18)"

Willow: A dramatic rounded shade tree with sweeping low branches that droop almost to the ground.

Add some panache to your wardrobe with this fashionable poncho-like accessory that features willow lace at the bottom and collar. The dramatic, intarsia I-cord insert makes this a timeless beauty.

Materials

Mosco from Schulana (67% viscose, 20% mohair super kid, 13% polyamid; 25 g; 125 m) **2**

A: 7 skeins in color 25 Kiwi

B: 1 skein in color 23 Wine

Size 9 (5.5 mm) circular needle (24") or size required to obtain gauge

Spare needle or large stitch holder

6 matching stitch markers

1 contrasting stitch marker

Tapestry needle

Gauge

22 sts = 4" in St st

Willow Edge Pattern

(Multiple of 10 + 5 sts)

Note: This pattern is also charted; see page 68.

Rows 1 and 2: Knit.

Row 3 (RS): P1, K2, *YO, K3, sk2p, K3, YO, K1, rep from * to last 2 sts, end K1, P1.

Rows 4, 6, 8, and 10: K1, purl to last st, K1.

Row 5: P1, K2, *K1, YO, K2, sk2p, K2, YO, K2, rep from * to last 2 sts, end K1, P1.

Row 7: P1, K2, *K2, YO, K1, sk2p, K1, YO, K3, rep from * to last 2 sts, end K1, P1.

Row 9: P1, K2, *K3, YO, sk2p, YO, K4, rep from * to last 2 sts, end K1, P1.

Rows 11 and 12: Knit.

Poncho

*With A, CO 45 sts. Work rows 1–12 of willow edge patt. Sl sts to holder or spare needle and cut yarn.

Rep from * 5 (6) times to make a total of 6 (7) panels, but *do not* cut yarn on last panel.

Joining rnd: K45 sts across panel on needle, with B, CO 4 sts, drop B and bring A across from previous segment (see "Working I-Cord Circularly" on page 68), K45 from next panel. Rep until all segments are tog on needle, pm to mark beg of rnd and join,

being careful not to twist sts—45 sts between each I-cord, 294 (343) sts total.

Cont in patt until piece measures 10 (11½)" from garter ridge at top of willow edge patt.

Dec rnd: (With A, K1, K2tog, knit to 3 sts before I-cord, ssk, K1, with B, K3) 6 (7) times.

Rep dec rnd every 6 rnds for a total of 3 times—39 sts between I-cords.

Rep dec rnd every 4 rnds for a total of 3 times—33 sts between I-cords.

Rep dec rnd every other rnd for a total of 7 (8) times—19 (17) sts between I-cords.

Next rnd: (*K3, K2tog, rep from * to last 4 (2) sts, K4 (2), sl marker, with B, K4) 6 (7) times—16 (14) sts rem between I-cords.

Work 4 rnds even.

With A, BO all sts.

Collar

With A, CO 35 sts. Work rows 1–12 of willow edge patt. Sl sts to holder or spare needle and cut yarn. Rep from * 5 times to make a total of 6 panels, but *do not* cut yarn on last panel.

Joining rnd: K35 sts across panel on needle, with B, CO 4 sts, drop B and bring A across from previous segment, K35 across next piece. Rep until all

segments are tog on needle, pm to mark beg of rnd and join, being careful not to twist sts—35 sts between each I-cord.

Cont in established patt for 4 rnds.

Dec rnd: (With A, K1, K2tog, knit to 3 sts before I-cords, ssk, K1, with B, K3) 6 times.

Work dec rnd every other row 8 times—19 sts rem between I-cords.

Work 1 rnd even.

Next rnd: (*K3, K2tog, rep from * to last 4 sts, K4, sl marker, with B, K4) 6 times—16 sts rem between I-cords.

Work 4 rnds even.

With A, BO all sts.

Finishing

Place collar on top of poncho with RS of collar facing out and aligning I-cord inserts. Sew in place neatly (see "Whipstitch" on page 75). Weave in ends. Block using mist method (page 76) to smooth and even the sts.

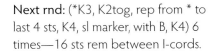

Green Thumb Tip

Working I-Cord Circularly

When working I-cord circularly, the yarn remains at the left side of work. Pull the yarn across the back of the work to the right side of the I-cord and knit the I-cord stitches. This will cause the I-cord to ride above the stockinette-stitch segments. A small ball of color B will be required for each I-cord insert. Color A is carried across the back of the I-cord; the same ball is used to work across all 6 (7) sections of body.

Elizabeth Zimmerman, credited as the inventor of I-cord (Idiot's cord), would probably name this piece "Idiot's Delight."

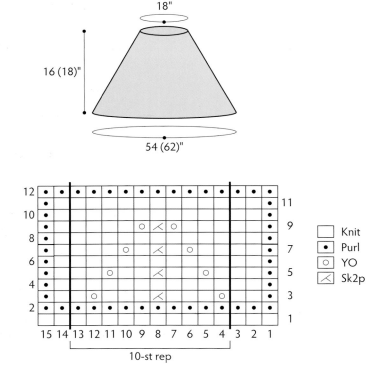

18"

16 (18)"

54 (62)"

		Knit
•		Purl
○		YO
⟋		Sk2p

10-st rep

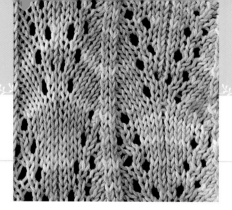

Zebra Grass

Sizes: Small/Medium (Large/Extra Large)
Finished Measurements: Length: 50 (50)" excluding rib and fringe
Width: 18½ (22½)"

Zebra grass: A strikingly exotic and graceful-looking ornamental grass with horizontal leaf striping.

Just as zebra grass is an excellent backdrop to any garden, this scarf with graceful gossamer fringe ends that flutter and wave in the breeze is gorgeous with any outfit. It features a grass lace pattern with a center-back seam that's the perfect finishing touch.

Materials

2 skeins of Ruca from Araucania Yarns (100% sugar cane; 100 g; 263 yds) in color 16 green/yellow (3)

Size 7 (4.5 mm) needles or size required to obtain gauge

Extra size 7 (4.5 mm) needle

Tapestry needle

Gauge

15 sts = 4" in zebra-grass patt

Gossamer Fringe Pattern

(Multiple of 3 + 2 sts)

Row 1 (RS): P1, K1-tbl, *P2, K1tbl, rep from * to end.

Row 2: P1, *K1-tbl, K1, P1, rep from * to last st, end K1tbl.

Rep rows 1 and 2 for desired length of fringe.

Row 3: P1, K1-tbl, *drop next st off needle and unravel to CO edge, P1, K1tbl, rep from * to end.

Rib Pattern

(Multiple of 2 sts)

All rows: *P1, K1-tbl, rep from * to end.

Zebra-Grass Pattern

(Multiple of 15 + 10 sts)

Note: This pattern is also charted; see page 72.

Row 1 (RS): K5, *ssk, K4, YO, K3, YO, K4, K2tog, rep from * to last 5 sts, K5.

Row 2: K5, purl to last 5 sts, K5.

Row 3: K5, *ssk, K5, YO, K1, YO, K5, K2tog, rep from * to last 5 sts, K5.

Row 4 and all even rows except 2 and 20: K5, *P7, K1, P7, rep from * to last 5 sts, K5.

Row 5: K5, *ssk, K3, YO, K2, p1, K2, YO, K3, K2tog, rep from * to last 5 sts, K5.

Row 7: K5, *ssk, K4, YO, K1, P1, K1, YO, K4, K2tog, rep from * to last 5 sts, K5.

Row 9: K5, *ssk, K2, YO, K3, P1, K3, YO, K2, K2tog, rep from * to last 5 sts, K5.

Row 11: K5, *ssk, K3, YO, K2, p1, K2, YO, K3, K2tog, rep from * to last 5 sts, K5.

Row 13: K5, *ssk, K1, YO, K4, P1, K4, YO, K1, K2tog, rep from * to last 5 sts, K5.

Row 15: K5, *ssk, K2, YO, K3, P1, K3, YO, K2, K2tog, rep from * to last 5 sts, K5.

Row 17: K5, *ssk, YO, K5, P1, K5, YO, K2tog, rep from * to last 5 sts, K5.

Row 19: K5, *ssk, K1, YO, K4, P1, K4, YO, K1, K2tog, rep from * to last 5 sts, K5.

Row 20: K5, purl to last 5 sts, K5.

Rep rows 1–20 for patt.

Scarf Half (Make 2.)

CO 68 sts.

Work rows 1 and 2 of gossamer fringe patt until piece measures 3".

Work row 3 of gossamer fringe patt—46 sts.

Work in rib patt for 2", ending with WS row.

Work inc as foll:

Row 1 (RS): K3, *M1, K4, rep from * to last 3 sts, K3—56 sts.

Rows 2 and 4: Purl.

Row 3: K3, *M1, K5, rep from * to last 3 sts, K3—66 sts.

Small/Medium only:

Row 5: K8, M1, K20, M1, K10, M1, K20, M1, K8—70 sts.

Row 6: Purl.

Large/Extra Large only:

Row 5: K5, *M1, K3, rep from * to last 4 sts, K4—85 sts.

Row 6: Purl.

All sizes:

Work in zebra-grass patt until piece measures 25", ending with row 20.

Knit 1 row and move to extra needle. Do not bind off.

Rep for second piece.

Finishing

Create center back seam: With RS tog, join using 3-needle BO (page 74). Fold in half lengthwise and seam underarm between ruffle and beg of garter edge (see "Mattress Stitch" on page 75). Weave in ends. Block using mist method (page 76) to smooth and even the sts.

Green Thumb Tip

To adjust the length, work more or fewer pattern repeats, but work the same number on each piece.

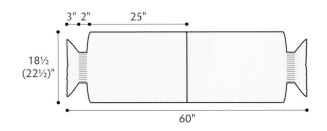

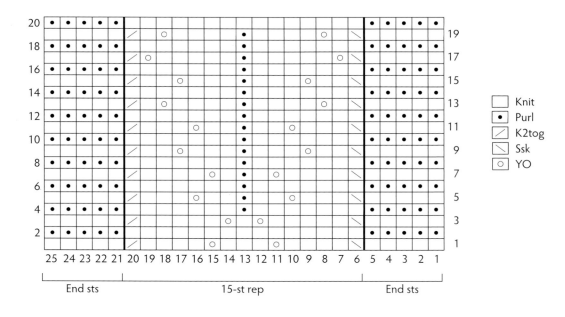

☐	Knit
•	Purl
╱	K2tog
╲	Ssk
○	YO

End sts   15-st rep   End sts

The following information on some of the techniques may introduce you to one that you have not encountered before or help you perfect your knitting skills.

Casting On

A pattern may specify a cast-on method that's different from your preferred method. Here are several methods that are used in this book.

CABLE CAST ON

Make a slipknot and place on a needle. Knit into the loop and place the resulting stitch on the left needle by inserting the left needle into the stitch from the right side of the loop. *Insert the right needle between the two stitches, wrap the yarn around the needle, pull the new loop through to the front, and place it on the left needle. Repeat from * for the specified number of stitches.

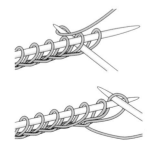

PROVISIONAL CAST ON

At times, when the cast-on edge is only a temporary edge and live stitches will be needed later, a provisional cast on works well. You can then join new knitting working in the opposite direction, graft live stitches together, or work an edging on your piece.

1. Use a crochet hook and make a number of loose chain stitches with a contrasting slippery yarn, such as a mercerized cotton. Make one chain for each stitch that will be cast on the needle plus a few extra.

2. Using a knitting needle, knit into the back of each chain with the project yarn. Begin knitting as instructed in the pattern.

3. To pick up the stitches, remove the crochet chain one stitch at a time and place the live stitches back on the knitting needle.

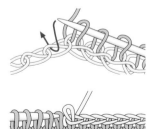

BACKWARD-LOOP CAST ON

This is an easy cast on whenever you need to add stitches within a row. *Form a loop with the end of the yarn in front of the needle. Insert the right needle into this loop and tighten gently. Repeat from * for the desired number of stitches.

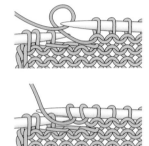

Joining a New Ball of Yarn

Whenever possible, attach a new ball of yarn at the beginning of the row. Tie the new strand onto the old tail with a single knot. Slide the new knot up the old tail to the needle and begin knitting with the new yarn. Weave in the tails as you finish the project.

Increasing

You have several choices when it comes to increasing stitches. The project instructions specify which method to use, and when, to achieve the same look as shown in the project.

YARN OVER (YO)

If the last stitch worked is a knit stitch, bring the yarn between the needles to the front. Take the yarn over the right-hand needle to the back; one yarn over made. If the last stitch worked is a purl stitch, the yarn is already in the front. Take the yarn over the right needle to the back; one yarn over made. Yarn overs are often paired with knitting or purling stitches to make open lacework without changing the stitch count.

MAKE ONE (M1)

Insert the right needle under the bar of yarn between the last stitch knit and the next stitch to be knit. Lift the bar onto the left needle and knit into the back of the stitch; one stitch made.

KNIT IN THE FRONT AND BACK OF STITCH (K1F&B)

Insert the right needle into the designated stitch on the left needle where the increase is to be made. Knit as usual, but do not slip the original stitch off of the left needle. Move the right needle behind the left needle and knit into the back of the same stitch. Slip the original stitch off the left needle—two stitches created from one stitch.

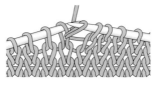

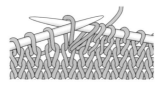

KNIT IN THE FRONT, BACK, AND FRONT OF STITCH (K1FBF)

Insert the right needle into the designated stitch in the left needle; knit as usual, but do not slip the original stitch off the left needle. Move the right needle behind the left needle and knit into the back of the stitch; do not slip the original stitch off the left needle. Reposition the right needle so that it's in the front of the left needle; knit the stitch as usual. Slip the original stitch off the left needle—three stitches created from one stitch.

Three-Needle Bind Off

Place half the stitches on one needle and half on a second needle. With right sides together, hold both needles in your left hand. Insert the right-hand needle into the first stitch on the front needle, and then into the first stitch on the back needle; knit the two stitches together. Repeat with the next two stitches on the left-hand needle; then bind off loosely in the usual manner. Continue knitting two stitches together from the front and back needles and binding off across the row. When one stitch remains on the right-hand needle, cut the tail and pass it through the last loop.

Seams

A few of the projects require seams to join the pieces. There are different ways to make seams, depending on what kind of stitches you're joining.

SEAMING VERTICAL STITCHES TO VERTICAL STITCHES

Work on the right side with wrong sides together and right sides facing out. Insert a tapestry needle threaded with matching yarn under the two strands forming the V that points toward the seam; pull the yarn through and repeat on the other side, working V to V across the seam. The seam should look like a row of knitting. Work carefully and do not pull the yarn too tight.

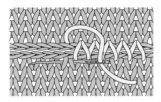

SEAMING VERTICAL STITCHES TO HORIZONTAL STITCHES

Work on the right side with wrong sides together and right sides facing out. Insert a tapestry needle threaded with matching yarn under the two strands forming the V that points toward the seam; pull the yarn through, and on the other side, insert the needle under one or two bars between stitches. Repeat until the seam is complete. Because there will be more bars than Vs, you will have to alternate the number of bars worked to make a smooth, flat seam. Generally there is a three-to-four ratio, meaning that working one bar and one V three times, and then working two bars and one V across the seam, should accommodate the difference.

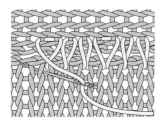

WHIPSTITCH

Hold pieces with right sides together and wrong sides facing out. Insert a tapestry needle threaded with matching yarn just inside the edge of the pieces, pull through, and bring the needle around to the front, ready to insert again. Repeat until the seam is complete, taking care not to seam too tightly. The yarn will appear wrapped around the edges of the pieces.

MATTRESS STITCH

The mattress stitch is a good choice whenever the side edges of pieces are joined, and when done correctly does not show. Align pieces side by side, with the Vs of the knit stitches pointing upward and aligned on both sides. Thread a tapestry needle with matching yarn. Insert the needle under the bar between the legs of the first stitch on one side, and then under the bar between the legs of the corresponding stitch on the other side. Pull tight, taking care not to pucker the seam. Continue as set, moving up the pieces and alternating sides, until the seam is complete.

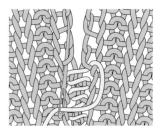

Blocking

First choose a flat, waterproof surface to spread out the piece to be blocked. Blocking boards can be purchased or the top of an ironing board or the floor covered with a towel will work, depending on the size of the project. Regardless of the method used for blocking, the piece should remain in place until dry.

MIST METHOD

Lay the knitted piece on the surface, shaping to the specified dimensions. Fill a clean spray bottle with water and mist lightly. Allow to dry completely before moving.

MIST-AND-PIN METHOD

Lay the knitted piece on the surface and pin the piece to the specified measurements. Fill a clean spray bottle with water and mist heavily. Allow to dry completely before removing pins.

WET BLOCKING METHOD

Dip the knitted piece in cool water. Gently squeeze out the water. *Do not* wring or twist the piece. Roll the piece in an absorbent bath towel to blot out the excess water. Spread on the surface and pin or insert blocking wires and pin to specified dimensions. Allow to dry completely before removing the pins or wires.

Applying Fringe

Cut the fringe to the specified length. Fold in half. Insert the crochet hook from the front to the back of the work. Catch the folded fringe and pull through the knitted piece, creating a loop. Draw the fringe ends through the loop and pull to tighten. Trim as necessary to even the lengths.

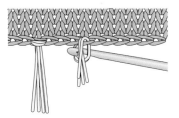

Crochet

You don't have to be a lifelong crocheter to add details and finishing touches to your knitted projects with these simple stitches. Pick up a hook and try it out—the results are worth it!

CHAIN STITCH (CH)

Wrap the yarn around the hook and pull through the loop on the hook.

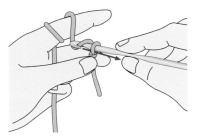

SINGLE CROCHET (SC)

Working from right to left with the right side facing you, insert the hook into the next stitch, wrap the yarn over the hook, pull the loop through the stitch to the front, wrap the yarn over the hook, and pull the loop through both loops on the hook.

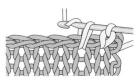

Insert hook into stitch, yarn over hook, pull loop to the front, yarn over hook.

Pull loop through both loops on hook.

DOUBLE CROCHET (DC)

Working from right to left with the right side facing you, wrap the yarn over the hook, insert the hook into the next stitch, wrap the yarn over the hook, and then pull the loop through the stitch to the front (three loops on hook). Wrap the yarn over the hook and pull through the first two loops on the hook (two loops remain on hook). Wrap the yarn over the hook and pull through the remaining two loops on the hook.

Yarn over hook, insert hook into stitch, yarn over hook, pull through to front.

Yarn over hook, pull through two loops on hook.

Yarn over hook, pull through remaining two loops on hook.

REVERSE SINGLE CROCHET (REV SC)

Reverse single crochet (also known as the crab stitch) gives the stitches a twisted appearance. The edge will be slightly raised, making a nice decorative finish for bound-off or cast-on edges. To work reverse single crochet, with the right side of the project facing you, insert the hook into the first stitch below the cast-on or bound-off edge, starting at the left end of your work. Wrap the yarn over the hook, pull the loop through the stitch to the front, wrap the yarn over the hook again, and pull through both loops on the hook.

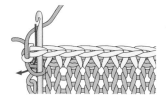

Join yarn with slip stitch. Insert hook into first stitch to the right.

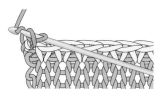

Yarn over hook, pull through both loops on hook.

KEEPING EDGES FLAT

It's important to space crochet stitches carefully so the edges of the piece lie flat. The formula for spacing stitches on a vertical edge is to work into each knot at the edge. For a horizontal row, the formula is one crochet stitch for every one and a half knit stitches. However, even using the formula as a guide, it may be necessary to skip or add stitches to keep the edge flat.

When working a crochet edge on a knitted piece, always begin by working a row of single crochet to stabilize the edges. To work additional rows of single crochet, insert the hook under both loops of the stitch below, and then work one single crochet into each stitch in the previous row.

Abbreviations

beg begin(ning)

BO bind off

C2B cable 2 back: skip the first stitch on the left needle, knit the 2nd stitch, leave on needle, knit the first stitch on the left needle and slip both stitches off needle

C2F cable 2 front: with right needle behind stitches, knit the 2nd stitch on left needle through the back loop, leave on the needle, knit first stitch as usual, slip both stitches off needle

C4B cable 4 back: slip 2 stitches to cable needle, hold in back, knit 2, knit 2 from cable needle

C4F cable 4 front: slip 2 stitches to cable needle, hold in front, knit 2, knit 2 from cable needle

ch chain

Cluster 3 slip 3 with yarn in back, move yarn to front, slip same 3 stitches to left needle, pass yarn to back, knit 3 (knit each of the 3 stitches slipped)

cn cable needle(s)

CO cast on

cont continue(ing)(s)

dc double crochet

dec decrease

dec 5 decrease from 5 stitches to 1: K2tog tbl, K3tog, pass stitch from K2tog tbl over stitch of K3tog

dpn double-pointed needle(s)

g gram

hdc half double crochet

inc increase(ing)(s)

K knit

K1f&b knit into the front and back of the next stitch

K1fbf knit into the front and back and front of the next stitch

K2tog knit 2 stitches together

K3tog knit 3 stitches together

LH left hand

M meter

M1 make 1 stitch

MB make bobble: (knit 1, purl 1, knit 1, purl 1, knit 1) into next stitch, turn, purl 5 stitches just made, turn, pass 2, 3, 4, and 5 stitches one at a time over first stitch, and then knit last stitch through the back loop

mm millimeter

oz ounce

P purl

P1f&b purl into the front and back of the next stitch

p2sso pass 2 slipped stitches over

P2tog purl 2 together

patt pattern

pm place marker

PU pick up and knit

rem remain(ing)

rev reverse

RS right side

s2kp slip 2 sts as if to knit, knit 1, pass the 2 slipped stitches over the knit stitch

sc single crochet

sk2p slip 1 stitch as if to knit, knit 2 stitches together, pass the slipped stitch over the knit stitch

sl 1 slip 1 stitch

sl1k slip 1 stitch knitwise

ssk slip, slip, knit

st(s) stitch(es)

St st Stockinette stitch (knit 1 row, purl 1 row; knit every row in the round)

tbl through the back loop

tog together

WS wrong side

wyib with yarn in back

wyif with yarn in front

yd(s) yard(s)

YO yarn over

Yarn-Weight Guidelines

Yarn-Weight Symbol and Category Name	**0** Lace	**1** Super Fine	**2** Fine	**3** Light	**4** Medium	**5** Bulky	**6** Super Bulky
Types of Yarn in Category	Fingering, 10-count crochet thread	Sock, Fingering, Baby	Sport, Baby	DK, Light Worsted	Worsted, Afghan, Aran	Chunky, Craft, Rug	Bulky, Roving
Knit Gauge Range* in Stockinette Stitch to 4"	33 to 40** sts	27 to 32 sts	23 to 26 sts	21 to 24 sts	16 to 20 sts	12 to 15 sts	6 to 11 sts
Recommended Needle in Metric Size Range	1.5 to 2.25 mm	2.25 to 3.25 mm	3.25 to 3.75 mm	3.75 to 4.5 mm	4.5 to 5.5 mm	5.5 to 8 mm	8 mm and larger
Recommended Needle in U.S. Size Range	000 to 1	1 to 3	3 to 5	5 to 7	7 to 9	9 to 11	11 and larger

*These are guidelines only. The above reflect the most commonly used gauges and needle or hook sizes for specific yarn categories.

**Lace-weight yarns are often knitted on larger needles and hooks to create lacy, openwork patterns. Accordingly, a gauge range is difficult to determine. Always follow the gauge stated in your pattern.

Resources

Alisha Goes Around
www.alishagoesaround.com
Daylily

Be Sweet
www.besweetproducts.com
Bean Sprouts

Berroco
www.berroco.com
Hyacinth

Claudia Hand Painted Yarns
www.claudiaco.com
Acorns

Dream In Color Yarn
www.dreamincoloryarn.com
Ostrich-Plume Fern

Knit One, Crochet Too, Inc.
www.knitonecrochettoo.com
Hop Vines

Knitting Fever
www.knittingfever.com
Bleeding Heart , Clematis, Roses, Zebra Grass

Lorna's Laces
www.lornaslaces.net
Red Beets

Louet
www.louet.com
Colorado Blue Spruce

Madelinetosh
www.madelinetosh.com
Brussels Sprout

Malabrigo Yarn
www.malabrigoyarn.com
Violets

Mountain Colors Yarns
www.mountaincolors.com
Maple Leaf

Plymouth Yarn Company Inc.
www.plymouthyarn.com
Ornamental Corn

S. Charles Collezione
www.tahkistacycharles.com
Pears

Skacel Collection, Inc.
www.skacelknitting.com
Willow

Tilli Tomas
www.tillitomas.com
Tulips

Acknowledgments

✳ Thanks to Gurney's Seed and Nursery Company and Gardens Alive! for sending their magnificent catalogs every January. Their spectacular garden photos sparked my creative process. Specifically, Scott, Jen, and Jen: thank you.

✳ Thanks to Cliff and Rosemary Bailey for the use of their picture-perfect farm for the photo shoot.

✳ Ruth and Ursula, thank you for sharing your masterful knitting skills.

✳ As always, many thanks to the entire staff at Martingale; you are all so talented.

✳ Of course, a special thank-you to my husband, Kevin, for tending the garden.